A Salesman Walks into a Classroom

The Art of Sales Meets the Science of Selling

PAUL D. BARCHITTA

iUniverse LLC
Bloomington

A SALESMAN WALKS INTO A CLASSROOM
THE ART OF SALES MEETS THE SCIENCE OF SELLING

iUniverse books may be ordered through booksellers or by contacting:

iUniverse
1663 Liberty Drive
Bloomington, IN 47403
www.iuniverse.com
1-800-Authors (1-800-288-4677)

ISBN: 978-1-4917-1882-7 (sc)
ISBN: 978-1-4917-1883-4 (hc)
ISBN: 978-1-4917-1884-1 (e)

Library of Congress Control Number: 2013923164

Printed in the United States of America.

iUniverse rev. date: 12/26/2013

Contents

Dedication

....

To my children Paul, Danielle, and Alexandra

Everything that I do, I do for you

To my wife Laura

who I met in a Geometry class in High School,

and have been in love with ever since. You have been there

every step of the way and I would have nothing without the

love and support that you have had for me over the past thirty years.

About the Author

Paul D. Barchitta is a Professor in the Maritime Transportation/ Business Department at the United States Merchant Marine Academy, located in Kings Point, NY. The U.S. Merchant Marine Academy is one of five Federal Service Academies including, West Point (Army), Annapolis (Navy), Air Force, Coast Guard, and Merchant Marine.

Prior to accepting this appointment, he was as a tenured faculty member for The City University of New York (CUNY) at Queensborough Community College. He has been a Professor at the following institutions in their respective Marketing/Business Administration Departments; SUNY College@ Old Westbury, Nassau Community College, Stockton College, Brooklyn College, LaGuardia Community College, Parsons School of Design, Wagner College, and St. John's University. He has also traveled to Taiwan on behalf of the American Education and Cultural Foundation to teach Marketing and Management.

He has a Post-Graduate, Advanced Certificate (30 Credits above an MBA) from a Doctoral program at NYU, in Corporate Training & Development. He has an M.B.A. in Marketing, and a B.S. in Finance from St. John's University. He is writing a dissertation on the correlation between relationship selling activities and the decision to purchase products; and the impact that this can have on sales.

He has over twenty years of sales experience in the Medical Device and Healthcare/Hospital industry. He has been a Field Sales Trainer and has sold a wide variety of medical products. Some of the product lines that he has sold are surgical stockings and lymphedema pumps that are prescribed for patients suffering from vascular disease, deep vein thrombosis equipment that prevents blood clots in patients during and post-surgery. Other lines have included general surgical instruments, spinal instruments, endoscopic, and laparoscopic instruments that are used in the operating room during surgery. Patient controlled analgesia pumps that regulate the amount of pain medication that a patient receives after surgery, and syringe pumps that are used to deliver small, precise doses of medication to premature infants. He has been a President's Club Winner for sales quota achievement for three global medical device manufacturer's including Johnson and Johnson's Surgical Instrument Division, Smith's Medical's Infusion Equipment Division, and Beiersdorf-Jobst's Vascular Division.

Introduction

Some people are born salespeople and others are not. I grew up in New York City and the furthest thing on my mind was a career in sales. It was not even close to being on the radar. As a youngster I had shown the academic ability to possibly attend medical school, but as they say, life gets in the way, and that career track went by the wayside. When I graduated from college I was not sure what I wanted to do. I had an athletic background, my father was a high school football coach, and we had connections everywhere. I went into the sporting goods business opening up a retail sporting goods store that catered to the institutional customer such as leagues, schools, and teams, specifically team uniforms, and other related sporting goods. I thought this was a natural fit for me, a sports store for a sports family.

This novelty ended quickly, what I did not realize was that it was more work than fun. I tried to do everything, and I mean everything, myself, to make the business successful. Every responsibility fell at my feet from being my own accountant, to being my own salesperson, and every other business function in between. Although it was a great experience because of the exposure that I had from every aspect of the business spectrum, I was frustrated with the accounting, finance, manufacturing, and production side of the business. I started to become more interested in the sales and marketing side of the business. I became passionate about hunting and finding the customer, and walking the customer through the entire process of closing the deal. Over time I wanted to shed myself of the non-sales related activities associated with the business so I sold the business and went into sales on a full-time basis.

I remember walking into my parent's home, during dinner, and telling them that I wanted to get into sales. I will never forget the look on my father's face, it was a look filled with disappointment, where he said to me, "You want to be a SALESMAN! Why did I send you to college?" Now, he has changed his tune and tone over time, but it is the negative connotation associated with a career in sales that drove me into university teaching, and the fundamental foundation behind the writing of this book. To change the negative perceptions associated with sales and salespeople. I am on a crusade to change this negative perception, does it still exist today? Of course it does. Do salespeople take advantage of customers and push them into purchasing products that they do not need? All day every day. My point is that you do not have to do that today. There is a more professional approach towards selling, and that is a purpose of this book, to expose salespeople to other methods of selling that can debunk the myth that all salespeople are evil and only interested in the commission that they are going to make on the sale.

After a few years of full-time selling I became interested in the sales training function of the organization. This led me to think about teaching sales at the university level. I walked into a lecture hall at a university filled with young doctors. Many companies practice the notion of orientating doctors when they are young because they can become users and prescribers of their products. It was a sales presentation to the doctors, but more of a lecture on what medical disorders my products could help cure. This was the day that the light went off in my head that I wanted to change my career path from selling to teaching and I have been on this crusade now for twenty years.

The book is designed to be used as a guidebook, handbook, and a reference point for all salespeople. The target audience for this book encompasses a wide range of sales professionals from entry level, to intermediate level, and even senior salespeople. Entry level salespeople who are new to selling as a profession need a handbook that they can reference as they begin their sales career. They need a blueprint that they can follow. Intermediate level salespeople who are possibly struggling to become successful might just need the confirmation that they are on the right track and need to build confidence in their approach to selling. Senior salespeople, who may have been trained as transaction salespeople, can benefit as well because old dogs can be taught new tricks in the game of sales. This book can act as a refresher course for even the most successful and seasoned sales professional.

The book commences with an overview of what the life of a salesperson is all about from finding your passion, to the freedom and independence that a career in sales can offer. Specific details and recommendations about time management, how to prioritize sales calls, where a career in sales can lead you, and how to prepare yourself to get the sales job that you want are all documented. Compensation and commission plans are addressed as well as the value of sales training, sales development, and the significance of ethical behavior among salespeople. The evolution from short-term transaction selling to long-term relationship selling is discussed as well as the magnitude of understanding who the customer is. A model of the steps in the selling process is outlined in addition to the importance of how to shorten the sales cycle. The book concludes with theories of sales motivation that can assist the salesperson develop a comprehension of the science of personal selling.

A career in sales can offer a salesperson more opportunity to advance within a company than people realize. Starting with a company in the sales department can provide a solid foundation that may present you with several different upward mobility career paths that can lead you all the way up the corporate ladder to CEO. The role of the salesperson is crucial to the overall success of an organization. Generating sales revenue and sustaining sales revenue were traditional roles. Current competitive trends in the industrial marketplace have rendered these roles increasingly less effective in establishing loyalty among buyers. There has been an underlying transfer in the theory and practice of corporate marketing. The role that the salesperson plays in establishing long-term loyalty among buyers needs to be redefined.

There are two basic questions that need to be answered in sales, who is my customer and why are they buying my product? It has become apparent that having a better understanding of the buying process and the behavior of customers can help the salesperson be more successful. Getting inside the head of the customer and thinking like the customer can enhance the ability of a salesperson, especially their ability to analyze the selling situation that they are in the middle of. To be successful is sales you have to be persistent, dedicated, and hard working. You need to be scientific in your approach, meaning you have to have a plan. You have to be robotic with your activity, every day you need to have a routine, you need to identify and follow steps that can lead you to success. You need to move your business forward every day, you need to accomplish something today that gets you closer to surpassing your quota.

The sales process can be defined as the steps that you need to follow from starting from scratch, or locating your potential customer, to approaching the customer, making a presentation to the customer, answering any questions or objections that they have, closing the sale, and following-up with the customer after the sale. If you follow these steps, and adhere to this model, you can be successful at selling. You need to know where you are going every day, you need to know where, and what stage of the sales process your customers are in. Every customer is at a different stage of the process, you need to be able to juggle this, know when to move to the next stage, and when to start the process over again with your next customer.

On the first day of every class, I ask the students what are their perceptions of salespeople? When you think of people who sell stuff to make a living, do you think of them in a positive or negative way? It is an overwhelming negative response. I ask them to open their mind and give me a chance to change that perception. I am on a crusade to change the negative perceptions associated with the life of a salesperson. This is what I am asking you to do as you read this book, place your previous preconceptions about sales and salespeople to the side, and look at selling from a different perspective. Today's professional selling approach emphasizes the development of a long-term relationship, compared to a short-term transaction. The pushy salesperson has been replaced by the problem solving salesperson. I believe in the problem solving approach to sales that is detailed in this book. Over the course of my career, I have developed a blueprint, or road map for sales success, that is detailed in the following pages and chapters. It can assist you in your quest to surpass your quota and achieve the financial goals that you seek in a career in sales. This method has worked for me, and I am not saying that it will work for everyone, but the story is worth reading about.

SECTION 1

Is Selling in Your DNA?

This section describes what the life of a salesperson is all about from a big picture viewpoint, with an overview of what a career in sales can offer, to specific daily activities that need to be followed in order to be successful at selling.

Chapter 1

The Life of a Salesperson:
It's a Wonderful Life

It's a Wonderful Life was a movie made more than a half century ago and the title can explain what the life of a salesperson can be. Sinatra crooned a song, *That's Life,* and if you read the lyrics it depicts the daily ups and downs that a salesperson goes through. I could not think of a more apropos compilation of words put to music that describe the life of a salesperson than the lyrics from *That's Life* which was written by Dean Kay and Kelly Gordon and brought to life by Frank Sinatra. If you do not see the correlation between the lyrics of this song and the life of a salesperson, then you have not been selling long enough, or maybe sales is just not for you. "I've been a puppet, a pauper, a pirate, a poet, a pawn, and a king." If you ask any salesperson if this can be applied to their life as a salesperson, if their answer is not yes to all, then they have not been selling long enough. "You're riding high in April, shot down in May, but I know I am gonna change that tune, when I'm back on top, back on top in June." This line accurately describes the roller coaster ride that is associated with the life of a salesperson. A career in sales is the ultimate amusement park ride. The roller coaster ride of ups and downs associated with the daily obsession of sales quota, did I make my quota today, this week, this month, this quarter, this half-year, this year, or whatever quota period the company has put in place?

3

A career in sales is not for everyone. If pay for performance excites you, and if you want to get paid for your effort and have an unlimited compensation plan based on how hard you work, and perform, then a career in sales is for you. If you are independent and want to control your life, a career in sales might be an option that you need to consider.

A career in sales is the ultimate double edged sword. What have you done for me lately is the mantra that you will hear from your sales manager every day. How do you deal with the psychology of selling is something that will constantly weigh on your mind as a salesperson. Quota never goes away, if you surpass the current quota goal you are always looking at the next quota period. This is a good thing, and something that can keep you motivated to achieve the financial rewards that you are looking for in a career in sales. It also can be and will be abused by sales management because they only look at salespeople in the light of what have you produced in the current quota period.

A career in sales is as unpredictable as any career. A salesperson wakes up on the first day of the year and has no idea what type of year it is going to be. This is different from what happens in the real world where you wake up on the first day of the calendar year and you can expect what your job is going to be like, what your compensation is going to be for the year. It is a very steady lifestyle. If that is not for you then a career in sales might be an option.

Finding Your Passion

You will spend so much time in your life going to work, it is imperative to find something that you love to do, not just like to do. It can take years for this light to go off in your head, but when it does you will know. If you can do something all day, every day, for hours a day, wake up the next day and do it again, and enjoy whatever it is and it does not feel like work, then you have found your passion. If you love what you do, and it does not feel like work, you have found that freedom and independence that can lead you to the promised land. Whatever the occupation, if you are passionate about it, and you thrive to become the best at that occupation, you probably can make a living at it.

Freedom and Independence

This is not a knock on the traditional nine to five Corporate America life, but after a while the ball and chain lifestyle of sitting behind a desk, regardless of compensation, can become tiresome, boring, and routine. Control is a magnificent mechanism to possess in life. Having control over your career through the freedom and independence that a career in sales can provide, is a viable option that should be considered. This does not mean that you will work less in a career in sales, but you can have more control of your career on a daily basis. There is something to say about your having the freedom of saying, "This is what I want to do today, and this is where I want to go today." It goes beyond the saying, "work smarter, not harder." There is one thing that must be made clear, there is no substitute for hard work, nothing will be given to you. Sometimes salespeople are the beneficiary of good fortune or good luck, but luck is the residue of hard work. There is nothing wrong with having a mentality of smart work meshed with a mentality of hard work.

The great sales managers want you as a salesperson in the field to think as an entrepreneur. This carved out piece of real estate, your territory that they have given you is yours. It is your business for you to run like an entrepreneur. You have been empowered to make business decisions, within the corporate framework, guidelines, and policies. In many ways you are in business for yourself, except that you have a corporate staff behind you. In many ways it is better than being in business for yourself because you do not have all of the responsibility that a business owner has, but can reap the benefits from your hard work and dedication. The best sales managers let you develop your own style of selling. At the end of the day you will be judged by your sales versus your quota and most managers do not care how you get to quota, they just care that you get to quota. Some salespeople prefer to use the phone to make appointments where others just show up. Some salespeople give detail oriented sales presentations, others do not. Again, whatever works for you and fits your style. This again fits neatly under the heading of freedom and independence to get the results that you and your sales manager are looking for.

Pay For Performance

A career in sales is not for everyone. If you want to punch a time card every day and can't wait for your shift to end, then sales is not for you. If you want to leave your job at 5pm and not think about your job until the next shift starts, then sales is not for you. If you want to leave your job on Friday at 5pm and not think about your job for the weekend, then sales is not for you. If you want to go on vacation and forget about your job, then sales is not for you. If you want a steady paycheck where you can budget what your compensation will be, then sales is not for you.

A career in sales is the ultimate pay for performance occupation. If you want a lifestyle where you are rewarded for your efforts, where the harder and smarter you work, the more compensation you can earn, then sales is for you. If you want your commitment and effort to be rewarded, then sales is for you. If you want to be remunerated for your persistence, creativity, and persuasiveness, then sales is for you. If you are challenged by the uncertainty of not knowing how much you will earn this year, and believe that you are in control of your destiny, then sales is for you.

If you want a nine to five lifestyle, then sales is not for you. If you want a twenty-four seven lifestyle, then sales is for you. This is not to say that you have to be on call every hour of the day, but it is a mentality that time is a precious commodity and you can be a productive salesperson any hour of the day, week, or year. Some days you might possess the motivation to work an eighteen hour day, and some days you might have this energy, but if you work hard and smart enough, you can be in control to adjust your life around your sales activity and productivity. This again, speaks to the notion of freedom and independence. There is no time clock and time cards in sales. It is a mentality. If making a sales call off-hours, or completing a sales report, or the planning that needs to be completed to finish a sales presentation takes place off-hours, so be it. It is all about pay for performance. If you know that your efforts can lead to compensation then who cares what time of day you work on the task. It is a mentality, and if this mind set interests you, then a career in sales may be a viable career path.

The Psychology of Selling

There is an absolute mental side or psychological effect that a life in sales can present. This contributes to the aforementioned roller coaster ride in this profession. You will find yourself scratching your head, talking to yourself, and at times wanting to bang your head against the wall. What can be frustrating is that you are wedged in the middle between the customer on one side and your sales manager and company on the other. Do you do the right thing by your customer or do you serve the needs of your sales manager and company?

On the corporate side there are multiple issues that can lead to the head banging and head scratching. Most companies put in place a tactical plan for a quota period, in this case, a calendar year. Most companies sell more than one product, so there can be an emphasis or focus on selling product "A" over product "B". What can direct your sales activity towards one product and away from another is the commission percentage that is placed on each product. For example, if the corporate focus is on product "A", a ten percent commission can be earned on all sales of product "A". Product "B" comes with a one percent commission on all sales. What if the sales cycle, or the amount of time it takes to target a potential customer or prospect is lengthy? You can exert your energy on generating sales of Product "A". What happens when at the end of the quota period when the tactical plan changes and now the better commission is on Product "C"? You just spent your time on Product "A" only to find out that when you wake up on the first day of the new quota period that your effort and energy was wasted? Get used to this as it is extremely common. Why would a company employ this shell game? It is possible that they are overstocked on inventory or components for Product "A", or the profit margin on this product is higher for the quota period in place. There can be countless reasons for this behavior, and do not ever expect to get a straight answer from your sales manager or company.

Companies can have all kinds of customers, in this example new customers or existing customers. At the start of this quota period the company can implement a relationship based strategy and compensation plan that rewards the sales person for increasing sales with current customers compared to generating sales with new customers. In this case the focus is on the type of customer and not the type of product. Sales to existing customers can be at ten percent while sales to new customers can be at five percent. So again, you toe the company line and guide your sales activity towards existing customers only to wake up at the commencement of the next quota period to find out that there has been a modification of the compensation plan with the newfangled strategy that concentrates on bringing in new business from new customers. Get used to this one as well.

Most companies provide a carved out geographical territory, usually defined by zip code. This is the best situation to be a part of. The worst situation to be a part of is where there are no geographical boundaries and when competitive sales people, often from the same company, who can be on your own sales team, steal leads or follow-up on inquiries made by prospective customers because you were spending time helping other customers.

The customary way to track sales is by what product has been shipped from a corporate headquarters into each zip code. Border wars can exist where territories butt up against each other especially in large metropolitan markets where there are multiple sales people in a given geographical area. It can become difficult to track where the actual sale was initiated and which salesperson deserves proper sales credit. Understand that corporate sales management is not concerned with which sales person receives sales credit for the sale. All that they are concerned with is that the sale was made and shipped from the corporate headquarters. Do not expect support from your sales manager either, because as long as the product was shipped into their geographical region, they receive sales credit to their region. Regional sales managers will only raise a concern when sales are being credited to regions outside of their geographical responsibility.

Another sore spot is when a product is shipped through distribution from the corporate headquarters, and then somehow ends up in your territory. Distribution partners are reluctant to provide tracking or tracing information about which products were shipped to which customers. This can be costly to the distributor with no benefit to the distributor. There is minimal motivation for the distributor to help the manufacturer track who is the end user of their product.

Another popular practice is to shuffle or change the actual geography of your sales territory. Again, this refers back to what is the strategic (long-term) and tactical (this year's) plan. If management is looking for an increase in customer penetration then they will hire and deploy more salespeople and put more boots on the street. If management is more concerned with bottom line expenses then they will cut back and condense territories and stretch the sales force across larger geographical areas.

This is where another sore spot occurs. It is all about developing relationships with customers, which will be detailed in the following chapters. Again, get used to the mentality of waking up on the first day of the year with the uncertainty of compensation hanging over your head. One of the first items to address is, "Okay, what customers am I going to target this year?" Once you identify who they are you then need to locate where they are. As you begin to map out where your prospects and customers are, you begin to piece a puzzle together of who to see and when to see them. You need to develop a route based on priority of customer needs and potential for sales.

Here comes another sore spot. It can take months or even years to develop the right relationship with a customer. What is meant by years, is that you can develop a relationship today with a customer and cultivate that relationship. That customer might not be ready or have a need for your product for some time. You need to stay in touch with that prospect until the time is right.

Most companies will play a shell game of shifting and modifying the geography of your sales territory. You can call on a customer all year only to wake up the next year to find out that your territory has been cut in half and a new salesperson will inherit the customers that you have been calling on. Once in a while a company will grandfather in customers that were taken away from you, but there is a ticking clock that will eventually expire. This one hurts especially when you have laid the foundation for a long-term relationship between your customer and your company only to have a new salesperson swoop in and reap the benefits of you hard work.

On the flip side you can experience the opposite situation where your geography can be expanded. This can be to your benefit because you can be the beneficiary of inheriting existing customers and prospects who might be interested in your product. For the record, the bigger and more expansive the geography the better, because more territory means more potential customers. The down side means more travel, and more time between customers. Travel can become an issue, family concerns about being on the road can become a concern. Remember time is money and the more time that you spend traveling from customer "A" to "B" is lost selling time. A smaller, concentrated geographical territory can add or enhance the practice of working smarter than harder. The challenge of the condensed territory is that over time you can saturate your territory and run out of potential prospects.

Today's trend is to have fewer, larger customers, coupled with the impact of mass distribution, companies would rather have one hundred huge customers than twenty thousand small customers. The biggest reason for the desire to have fewer, larger customers is that it is easier to manage one hundred massive customers than twenty thousand miniscule customers. Financial, accounting, and customer service reasons lead the way, it is easier to collect money and serve the needs of one hundred customers compared to twenty thousand. Throw in the impact that technology has had on the life of a salesperson. You are more virtual than physical. You can manage and service your accounts virtually. This has led to an increase in the size of geographical territories. The point is to get used to the geographical shifts from small territory to big, from big to small, then small back to big, it is all part of the life of a salesperson. Quota never leaves your mind, "How am I going to make my quota, how are my sales to date versus quota, for this month, this quarter, this quota period?" Understand that an increase in geographical territory can be associated with an increase in quota. More geography means more travel, which means more planning and better routing of your time. If your product requires more customer interaction and more face-to-face time with your customer, you can reach a point where you are spread too thin between customers. The geographical size of your territory can compromise your relationship with all of your customers.

Chapter 2

The Day to Day Life:
What to Expect Today

Time Management

Time is a precious commodity that needs to be cherished. Time is money and in no other profession is it more important than in the life of a salesperson. The quota clock starts ticking the first second of the quota period and never stops ticking. The first thing to comprehend is that you will waste a lot of time as a salesperson. If wasting time irritates you, or frustrates you, then sales might not be for you. You only have so much time and when you factor in other responsibilities that will cut into your selling time you will really appreciate the commodity that it is. Windshield time is the time driving in your car between sales calls. The bigger the geography the more time you will spend driving. If driving a car is not something that you are particularly fond of then a career in sales may not be for you. If driving in traffic bothers you this can be another issue. The bigger the geography the more windshield time, the more condensed of a metropolitan area, the more traffic. You will become immune to driving in traffic over time. Salespeople and sales managers who spend a significant time in airports flying to meet customers also become immune to the time waiting in an airport to board a flight. The key is to be productive during all of this downtime because any minute wasted is a minute that you could be selling.

You will need to travel to national, regional, and local corporate sales meetings during the year. This is time where you are taken out of the field to review the company's strategic sales plan, learn about products that may be introduced, review and reward the past year's sales achievements, and build teamwork and camaraderie among the sales force.

Sales training exercises will also take you out of the field. Even seasoned, veteran salespeople are required to participate in these exercises that can train you on a new product or a new software program that is being implemented throughout the company. Trade shows, where industries convene to discuss industry trends, introduce new products, network among colleagues, and meet potential and existing customers, will also take you out of the field. Throw in holidays, vacation days, personal days, sick days, and bad weather days where you cannot travel, and you can see that the three hundred and sixty-five day calendar can have more selling days shaved off of the calendar than you realize.

When is a good time to sell? Are there better times than others to sell, absolutely? Are there more advantageous times during the day, are there days that are more appealing during the week, during the month, or times during the year? Yes to all.

Early in the day has advantages, customers are fresh, have not been aggravated by the daily activity associated with their job. Too early might not be great, you want them to have a chance to settle into their day, so mid-morning is optimal. Late morning can become a challenge, customers get hungry and look forward to having their lunch. A meeting scheduled right before lunch might not give you enough time, plus the customer might rush your presentation if it infringes on their lunch time. After lunch is better, but give them a chance to get back into the flow of their day. Mid-afternoon is better. Late afternoon is tough because they have work that they want to finish before the end of their day, and their mind can start to drift out the window, thinking about their evening.

What days are more attractive than others? Monday morning is a challenge; customers are coming off the weekend and want to slowly start their week. The same goes for Friday afternoon. Customers can check out mentally, especially if it is during the time of year when the weather is favorable, or if the customer has plans for a special weekend. When is prime time? Tuesday at ten AM or Thursday at two PM is prime time. There is an exception to this is rule. Key decision makers and top management often work more hours than office staff, so they can be available for early morning or late afternoon/early evening meetings. Their urgency to meet with you will dictate how and when they fit you into their schedule, and you need to have the flexibility to accommodate their hectic schedule.

Do certain months or times of year provide a better atmosphere than others, yes? Winter can be tough in certain parts of the country, especially if it becomes a long winter that never seems to end. Hope springs eternal, and as the weather warms up, customers can warm up too. Summer time is notoriously slow for many industries. Customers take vacation and when one comes back, someone else in the decision making process goes away, stretching the sales process. Fall is appealing because customers are back from vacation, and may have funding in their budgets that they need to drain before the end of the year. The last two weeks of the year are the most difficult weeks of the year to sell anything that is not a holiday related product. Often you will hear, "Call me after the first of the year", which is a polite way of saying, "Don't bother me until January."

Weather can influence your activity in the field. There is nothing more beautiful than a blizzard that can create some very picturesque scenes. Driving in the snow is not a shrewd endeavor. It is dangerous and you can be placing your life in your hands. This issue is that even if you brave the elements and make it in to see a customer, you may find out that your customer stayed home because of the inclement weather. So snow is bad. Rain is also dangerous to travel in. If you show up rain drenched in front of a customer, it might compromise your professional appearance. So rain is not easy to sell in. Cold weather can be tough, especially brutally cold weather. You may need to walk a long distance between your car and your customer, which can happen when you are calling on a large customer complex such as a hospital. So cold weather is tough. Hot weather will drain you physically, in the car, out of the car, will take its toll. Plus as with the rain, showing up to make a sales call drenched in sweat is not very professional. So hot weather presents a problem.

When is the best day to be out in the field selling? In the middle of the week, Spring or Fall, beautiful sunshine, seventy degrees, at ten AM or two PM. If you add up that up, how many days does that equate to? It is not that many. Incorporate the aforementioned non selling days listed above associated with corporate travel, and personal time off. You can see how you are on the clock when it comes to maximizing your time to exceed your inflated, unrealistic, quota. The only way possible is to fight through the weather challenges where you will find yourself working in an unfavorable or undesirable environment.

One thing that is an absolute and a guarantee is that customers will waste your time. You need to become a better manager of your time. Customers take their time and they need to think about making the decision to purchase your product. Some customers need more time than others. Salespeople need to be patient and not push the customer, because the salesperson's quota clock does not pertain to the customer. Salespeople need to understand that as precious as time is to you, your time means nothing compared to the customer's time. They may be busy at work and have more pressing issues that need to be resolved before they can consider making the decision to purchase your product. You are there to serve their needs and need to be available when they are ready to purchase your product, not when you are ready to make the sale.

Fortunately, in the information technology world that exists today it has become easier to manage your time today as a salesperson. The life of a salesperson for the most part was a physical, face-to-face encounter. Picture in your mind the life of a door-to-door salesperson physically knocking on the door of a prospective customer. This still does exist, but the physical sales call has been supplanted by the virtual sales call. Today it is common for salespeople to spend one third of their time in front of a customer. What are salespeople doing with the other two thirds of their time? Traveling to and from customers, preparing for sales calls, phone calls, emails, text messages, sales reports, placing and following up on sales orders, all fill up the remainder of your time.

How you manage your time has never become more paramount in the daily life of a salesperson. Always keep in the back of your mind that at some point on most days a customer will waste your time. You can have a scheduled appointment at ten AM, and when you arrive you find out that your prospect is busy and has asked you to return at two PM. How do you handle this situation? What if it took you two hours to travel to see this prospect? If you hang around and wait until two PM then you just burned a half day of prime selling time.

No one is saying to start to believe in Murphy's Law, but expect your day to fall apart. Travel time between customers, traffic, weather, customer meetings that take longer than expected, waiting for customers, and other customer emergencies that need to be addressed during the day all can slow you down. Sure, you can relax and have a nice lunch and come back when your customer has more time to see you at two PM. No one is saying to starve yourself, but you can be productive during this down time. If possible try to have a backup prospect or customer that you can call on if something comes up with your solid appointment. If not, always have some other work that you can do while you have to wait for your meeting to start. It could be a weekly expense report, customer call report which documents your sales activity, sales forecast report, or just return phone calls, or emails to customers, your sales manager, or corporate contacts at your company's headquarters. The point is to do something with the time that you have been afforded. Remember, the weekly and monthly reports have to eventually get done, so why not get a head start on them while you are waiting for your customer.

The toys and tools that are available today include smart phones, tablets, laptops, and software programs that are all designed to save time and make you more efficient. Every minute that you save using the technology that is at your fingertips is a minute that you can be selling. It was not that long ago when salespeople had to hand write all of their reports, everything from expense reports to sale's forecasts. Before smart phones, there were car phones, and before that there were pay phones. In the pay phone generation you had to stop what you were doing to find a pay phone, and stay stationary while you called customers, or called your sales manager, burning precious sales time. Then the car phone was introduced, while wired into your car, at least you could be moving, and talking at the same time, hopefully hands-free. Today with a smart phone there are no boundaries for communication. The advent of technology and the personal computer changed all of this forever. Take a look at this through a time management prism. A weekly expense report required entering expenses on a form, making copies of all of your receipts, and snail mailing them to your sales manager or headquarters for approval. Today those entries are entered on a spread sheet, the receipts are scanned in, and many companies will accept a credit card statement that itemizes expenses, saving more time. That report can be emailed to your sales manager or headquarters for approval and the reimbursement process can begin immediately.

Expense report reimbursement that would take several weeks to be received and approved, can now be completed in days. Even if you had the most generous expense account, you would have had to incur the expense and wait for the reimbursement. Today the reimbursement process has been accelerated. Remember it is your money that you have to lay out to incur the expense. The faster that you submit the expense report the faster you are reimbursed. Previously it could take more than one hour per week to complete this report. With today's technology this report can be completed in less than thirty minutes.

Sales call reports document where you are spending your daily activity and can explain where you are going today and where you are going tomorrow. These were also hand written and now can be submitted electronically. Sales forecasting reports also follow this time saving format.

Two of the biggest time savers are how customer account records are kept and how orders are placed. Customer account records which list all information about an account including name, address, phone number, and account number all were hand written on big index cards or full size sheets of paper kept in binders. You could list key contact names, detailed notes of key points of discussion during your meeting, items that needed to be followed up on, the next steps in the sales process, and dates for future meetings. All of this arduous and primitive method of managing your contacts and accounts has been replaced by contact management software. Using any device including a smart phone, tablet, or laptop you can now access and enter account information at your fingertips on a moment's notice. Sales management loves this tool, but they have an ulterior motive. Yes, they will encourage you to utilize this tool to help manage your time, but their motive is to have updated account records. If you leave the company to pursue another opportunity, the salesperson who replaces you will not have to start from scratch and the learning curve of where to go and who to see can be accelerated.

The placing of sales orders has also been revolutionized. Hand written orders and phoned in sales orders have been replaced by electronic ordering as well. If it was an important or urgent sales order you might have called in the order to your company to insure it was received, placed, and that it was correct. You might want to record a confirmation number and delivery date and report this information back to your customer. All of this took time, now with software programs and technology such as Electronic Data Interchange (EDI), where computers talk to other computers, all of this can be handled electronically. Time on the phone or playing phone tag with customers has been reduced with the use of emailing and text messaging. Yes, the society in which we live in is being threatened by the lack of physical and voice communication, but all of this has made the salesperson more efficient. Customers will be more likely to respond to an email before they return a phone call, they are busy too, and it is easier for them to utilize the technology as well. Start adding up the time that is saved today, and before you know it, a few minutes here and there start adding up to more available selling time.

Big Brother

A downside of this technology is the opportunity for Big Brother to be looking over your shoulder. Field salespeople are a different breed, and generally rebel against the traditional nine to five corporate structure. That is a major reason why they become salespeople; again back to the freedom and independence mind set. A potential downside to all of the tools and toys that are at your fingertips is the aspect of sales management and headquarters using the technology to closely micro-manage your daily activity. For example, smart phones that are issued from a corporate headquarters have the ability to track the origin of your cell phone calls. They might not be able to pinpoint your exact location, but they can locate the cell area where you are calling from, and if you are making calls outside of your geographical territory during traditional business hours it can become an issue. If you are accessing your company's intranet (internal email system) from your office at home during normal selling time, when you should be out in the field too often, it can become an issue. EZ-Pass is an incredible technology that has eased traffic across bridges and highways, but is also provides a nice and neat statement that itemizes where you are and what time you cross a toll. Most pharmaceutical companies have equipped their sales people with wireless tablets and laptops that require them to login to the company intranet and obtain a signature from a physician when they dispense a sample. Another method of Big Brother looking down on salespeople.

For the record, all of these toys and tools are great because anything that can help you become more efficient in managing your time and helping you to close more sales is beneficial. There is nothing wrong with a big brother. If he helps you manage your time better to get you to become more efficient as a salesperson. The question is, would you want to work for a sales manager or company who can employ these Big Brother tactics and practices where your activity becomes more imperative than your production?

Routing

A perk in the life of a salesperson is that you are in control of where you work on a daily basis. You need to become exceptional at planning where you go today and where you go tomorrow. Routing, or figuring out where you are going, from point "A" to point "B" to point "C" to point "D", is a task that you need to master to maximize your selling time in the field. In the illustration below you have four customers that you need to see today. Let's qualify this by stating that there is no difference in the size of each customer, urgency, importance, and order that you see today. Which customer do you see first? Which customer do you end your sales day with?

Exhibit #1 Routing

ROUTING D-C-B-A

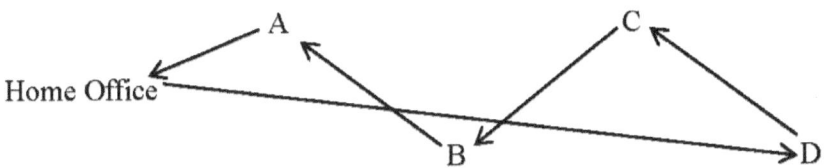

ROUTING C-B-A-D

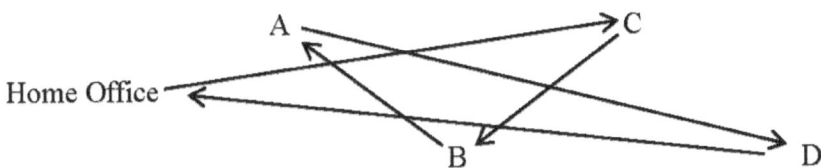

ROUTING B-C-A-D

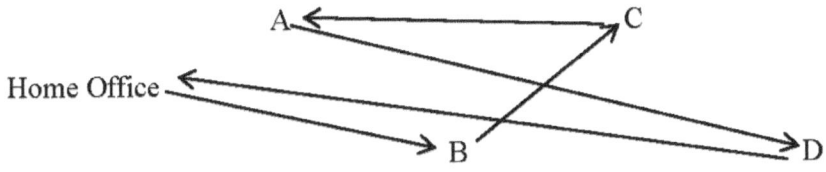

ROUTING A-B-C-D

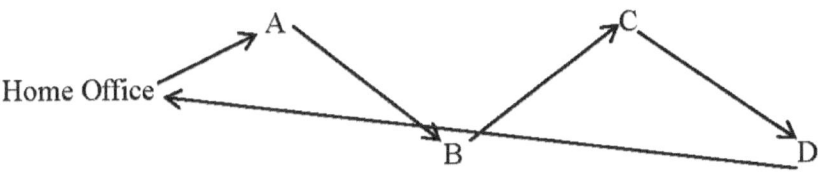

Crisscrossing across your territory (See Exhibit #1) with a route of C-B-A-D, or B-C-A-D makes no sense and can have you spinning your wheels and chasing your tail all day. If your route is customer A-B-C-D, then yes, you can get an early start and see customers very early in the day. The downside is that when your day is over after your sales call on customer "D", you are the furthest distance from your home office and then face the traffic that is associated with this.

Consequently, a route of D-C-B-A can make more sense for a few reasons. Get an early start to stay ahead of the morning rush hour, you have more energy, and are fresher in the morning, plus get the most amount of driving out of the way early in the day. You can also travel out the night before, stay overnight, and start your day near your first customer. Let's say that you spend the same amount of time with a route of A-B-C-D than you do with a route of D-C-B-A. When you finish the A-B-C-D route you are at the end of the day, and are at the end of your geographical territory. You now have the most driving that you have had to do all day still ahead of you, and have to travel all the way back across your territory to get to your home office. If your route is D-C-B-A, at the end of the day you are at the customer who is the closest to your home office, with the least amount of driving for the day ahead of you. Keep in mind that upon returning to your home office you may need to follow up with phone calls, emails, and sales reports so you want to have the most efficient day possible out in the field.

Prioritizing Sales Calls

There are many sales jobs where you are recruited, hired, and trained and then thrown to the wolves (customers) with your sales manager telling you to go ahead figure it out. This is not bad, this is actually the type of selling situation that you want to be thrust into, where you are allowed to develop your own style of selling, and you are empowered to run your sales territory as if it was your own business.

Let's say that you have one hundred prospects and existing customers in your carved out geographical territory. The sales for your territory are one million dollars, and are the sum of all of the sales of the customers in your territory. Your quota for next year is ten percent over the sales from the previous year, or one million, one hundred thousand dollars. Where do you go today? Who do you visit tomorrow? Where do you go next week? Next month? How often or how infrequently do you make a sales call on a customer or prospect?

A sales call can be defined as a visit by a salesperson to a potential or existing customer with the intent to sell a product. Some sales calls can last five minutes and some can last five hours. How does a sales call last five minutes? What if a customer is in need of a sample of your new product, but when you arrive they inform you that the only have five minutes of time, thank you for the sample, and agree to schedule more time in the future to talk about the sample. That is a five minute sales call that was productive. How does a sales call last five hours? You arrive for an appointment at eight AM, and your customer tells you to just wait a few minutes. They tell you that it will be only a few more minutes, and before you know it they tell you to come back at twelve noon. You find another way to be productive. Before you know it you get the time that you have been waiting for and close a deal by one PM, that's a five hour sales call. Remember these are your decisions about where to go and spend your time, and not your sales manager's, or company's, yet you are responsible to deliver the established sales quota of one million one hundred thousand dollars.

Eighty/Twenty Rule

It is normal to look at that quota and be intimidated. How do you get every customer to buy what they bought last year, not lose any of your customers to your competitors or attrition, and also grow the total dollar amount of your territory by ten percent or one hundred thousand dollars? There is a theory in marketing called the eighty/twenty rule. What it means is that eighty percent of your sales will come from twenty percent of your customers. Using the one hundred customer example this means that twenty of your customers will purchase in total eight hundred thousand dollars of your company's product from you. The remaining eighty customers will only purchase two hundred thousand dollars total. If you average that out it means that you will have twenty huge accounts and eighty small accounts. The twenty huge accounts (Top Twenty) average forty thousand dollars in sales each, or eight hundred thousand dollars in annual sales. The eighty smaller accounts (Lower Eighty) will purchase on average only twenty-five hundred dollars in sales or two hundred thousand dollars in annual sales. This means that you have to manage a handful of large customers and have too many small, perhaps insignificant customers.

Customers on the surface all can look like great prospects. But as you begin to dig deeper into the prospecting and qualifying, or as you peel the onion back, you can begin to separate a prospect from a suspect. All companies are run differently, some are managed well and others are managed poorly. A customer has to have a need for a product and the financial ability to pay for a product. You can have a great product that can satisfy a customer's need, and solve their problem, but if your product is too expensive, you can be shut out of the opportunity. You need to qualify your prospects, separate who has the ability to pay for your product and who does not. This can be a reason why a company is a top twenty account and why another falls into the lower eighty. On the surface you can have two customers that are competitors, but one specializes in one area of their business compared to the other. What if your product meets their needs and the other customer does not have as much of a need for your product? That alone can push one customer into the top twenty and another into the lower eighty. One customer can be targeting one demographic, or focusing on a specific niche in the market, and can create the demand or lack of demand for your product. This again effects their ranking in your top one hundred accounts. The point is, there are several reasons why an account is a top twenty account or a lower eighty account.

Here is the formula that you need to follow. The eighty/twenty rule works and does have merit. You need to attack your territory and have a targeted focus. Keep in the back of your mind that the quota clock is ticking. Focus is the key. Focus on the top twenty accounts. To make this example clean and neat, assume that all of your customers added up purchase the exact same amount of your company's product that was sold the previous year, some purchase a little more, some purchase a little less. You still need to increase sales by ten percent or one hundred thousand dollars. How do you spend your time, and which customers do you solicit to increase your territory's sales to help achieve your quota? You can call on all one hundred accounts and spread yourself thin. Following the eighty/twenty rule, just focus on the top twenty accounts. You have a better chance of increasing the sales of your top twenty accounts from eight hundred thousand dollars to nine hundred thousand dollars, than you do of increasing the sales of your lower eighty accounts from two hundred thousand dollars to three hundred thousand dollars.

There is a reason why they are a top twenty account. They could have had a relationship with the salesperson that preceded you, or an established history with your company or product. It really does not matter, something is working. This is your task, to continue the relationship with this customer, and take it to the next level, which is to satisfy their needs and increase their sales.

The flip side applies. There is a reason why this customer is a lower eighty account. It can be many reasons. They have a relationship with a salesperson who is your competitor, or a long history with their company or product, and there is some loyalty there which is fine. As a new salesperson you might not have the same relationship that your competitor has with your customer. They can have no prior, or a limited history with your company or product.

It all comes back to time management and how well you manage your time. Should you give an equal amount of time to all of your customers? The answer is no. You should spend eighty percent of your sales time on your top twenty customers. Therefore, twenty percent of your time should be spent on the lower eighty accounts.

Most companies will set guidelines for the average amount of sales calls that you should be making in the field every week. Size of the territory can make a difference, the complexity and length of a sales call can make a difference. They set a goal for the average number of sales calls you should make per week. Using twenty-five sales calls as an average, means that you should make twenty sales calls to your top twenty accounts every week, which is one sales call per week. This can be necessary based on the volume of sales that you receive from these top accounts, which average forty thousand dollars per year. That leaves five sales calls per week for the lower eighty accounts. This equates to approximately three to four sales calls per year or once a quarter. You can split the lower eighty as well. For some accounts you only make a sales call twice a year or even just once a year to stay in contact. Remember there is a reason why they are at the bottom of your list, and your time is better spent pursuing other opportunities. Customers at the top of your lower eighty account list should always be kept an arm's distance away because something can always change that can thrust them into your top twenty. In the near future they might require more attention from you.

Telecommuting

The secret is out, the cat is out of the bag, the horse has left the barn, and the rest of Corporate America has discovered the beauty of working from home. An estimated twelve percent of the U.S. workforce conducts most of its work away from the company office, with this figure forecast to rise by forty percent by 2012[1]. Now that figure may sound high but it is somewhere in between, with the point being that the amount of workers telecommuting today is on the rise. Forever, working from home has been the base and headquarters for the career salesperson. A dollar amount cannot be computed to compare the benefits of working from home, compared to working in the corporate headquarters structure. The first issue that must be addressed is that just because you work from home does not mean that you work less, it just means that you are in more control of when your work is completed. You still have the same amount of work that must be completed from Monday morning through Friday afternoon, but you are in control of when the work is completed. Some people like to work hard early in the week, which can free time up by the end of the week. Some people want to ease into the week and finish up strong. Some people like to work early in the day and free up the rest of their day. Some people are night owls and are more productive into the wee hours. The point is that there is flexibility and control that can enrich the freedom and independence associated with a career in sales where telecommuting is your base.

Most companies have a domestic U.S. headquarters that can be located anywhere. Most companies, depending on the size of revenue, will deploy salespeople throughout the country, usually based somewhere around a metropolitan area or market. If a company has fifty sales people they are typically based in the fifty biggest markets. It is common to have multiple salespeople in the largest metropolitan areas such as New York City, Los Angeles, and Chicago.

The toys and tools (technology) that are available today can replicate the corporate headquarters environment. Desk-top computers, laptops, and tablets can all be set up at home. Printers, copy machines, fax machines, and scanners have all been crammed into one device! Second or office phone lines that now combine phone, Internet, and television service have become the norm. All of these toys make it easy set up your office at home. In most corporate office jobs there is some commuting that is involved. Understand that the time you spend getting to and from work is not part of your compensation. The time that you spend in the car, on the bus stop, on the train, waiting for the bus or train, or sitting in traffic is your personal time. When you are telecommuting you are working from your home. If you have a nine AM meeting, you can roll out of bed at eight fifty-five, fire up your device, connect to your company's intranet and be productive within minutes of rolling out of bed. You cannot put a price on that.

The freedom and independence of telecommuting can enhance the work life balance that you desire. If you have personal commitments that take you away from your desk a few hours during the day, so be it; you can make up the time, either earlier that day, or later in the evening. There is no time clock when you telecommute. You have a certain amount of work that must be completed by a certain deadline, and it is your responsibility to meet that deadline. Some people find this refreshing, some people can struggle with this.

The struggle comes with being conditioned to the corporate headquarters lifestyle, that you have to be at your desk by a certain time, take a timed lunch hour and stay until five PM. The struggle occurs because you have to dress professionally, and have to look over your shoulder all day. This does not exist with telecommuting. Unless you have to participate in a webinar, where there is a webcam on you, when you telecommute you can wear whatever suits you for the day. You can take lunch on your timetable for as long as you want. The work needs to be done, so if you want to indulge yourself with an extended lunch hour, the work will be there when you return. Another struggle is keeping work separate from your home life. When you leave the corporate office, you can leave your work there and enjoy the time away with your family or doing something that you want to do. There is a distinct separation between work and life outside of work. When you telecommute and your office is in your home it is difficult to separate your home life from your work life. The office that you have set up in your home can act like a huge magnet that has the power to pull you in any time of the day or week. You can find yourself drifting into your office in the evening if nothing interests you on television, or stopping in on a weekend morning while waiting for a family activity to start. If this temptation bothers you, then stay in the corporate structure. If this entices you, pursue a career that allows you to telecommute. When you telecommute it is difficult to make the separation from your home life and work life.

The latest trend to hit telecommuting actually takes telecommuting to the next level. At first when this concept was introduced you could duplicate your office setting at home. Your desk-top personal computer was wired to your home, and your Internet connection, while remote, was anchored in your home office. Now as a result of wireless technology, you can take your laptop, tablet, or smart phone on the road anywhere you go, hence the term, mobile telecommuting. When you were wired at home your company could actually track when you were logged into your company's intranet. They can monitor when you were online and when you were not. It is a given that salespeople do need to spend time in their office completing reports, reviewing sales orders, and sales trends from customers that can be accessed remotely. You need to be out in the field. If you are underperforming, one of the first things to check is how much time are you spending in your office? Today you can access all of this information from your devices in the field. It has become more difficult for your sales manager to pinpoint where you are every day. Yes, as mentioned, EZ-pass provides a nice, neat statement of what highways and bridges you have crossed. The next wave of monitoring will come in the form of GPS in your devices, where they will be able to at least narrow down where you are on a daily basis.

Telecommuting is not for everyone. You need to have a strong, self-starter work ethic. Working from home can reinforce negative tendencies, it will facilitate a workaholic to work harder and longer, and it will give a procrastinator ample opportunity to delay work[2]. No one is looking over your shoulder to see if you arrived on time, came back late from lunch, or left early for the day. Some people need the discipline and structure. Other self-starter components are dealing with the distractions of being at home include a spouse, family, friends, something interesting on television, other chores around the house, and even a nice sunny afternoon. All of these components can distract you from your work. Yes, you can indulge in some of these distractions, but remember the work does not go away. For every minute that you are distracted during the work day is a minute of work that needs to be made up during non-traditional work hours. Some people struggle with this, others embrace it, and enjoy the break during the work day and welcome the non-traditional work lifestyle.

With all of the advantages and disadvantages associated with telecommuting, there are benefits and reasons why your company will ask you to clean out your desk and send you home to telecommute. They are not doing it because they want to be known as a nice place to work, although the enhanced work-life benefits can allow you to have a healthy balance between your work and your life outside of work. Happy workers are more productive workers, and if you are happier and more productive working from home then clean out your desk and head home. Before the trend of telecommuting became in vogue, a company was relegated to their local market for the talent pool of potential job candidates. Yes, a company can do a much broader geographical search, which is more costly, and involves a relocation package that is also expensive. Today, with the technology associated with telecommuting and the virtual office, the candidate can literally reside anywhere. The advantage of this is that it opens up a much bigger pool of potential job candidates. You can recruit and hire more talented and experienced employees who physically might not reside, and do not have to reside, in the backyard of the corporate headquarters.

Telecommuting was reserved for salespeople in the field, but today because of the connectivity between a headquarters and an employee's home, you are finding traditional nine to five Corporate America office jobs being shifted to the home. At one time there was a negative stigma associated with working from home. It was a sense of legitimacy, "How serious can your business be if your office is in your home?" The ivory tower, cosmetic corporate structure also leaned this way by physically impressing customers and employees by the size of the corporate structure. This mentality has gone by the wayside.

All of this costs money and can be expensive to maintain. The address was important. In New York City, if you were in the financial services industry you needed to have a shiny Wall Street address to lend credibility to your company. Today that has become insignificant, Wall Street is a shell of what it once was physically. Many of the physical stock brokerage houses that occupied lower Manhattan have moved, many across the river, to a cheaper place, to set up shop in New Jersey. Many have become virtual offices with stock brokers making their daily trades from their own home office.

Expense and technology are the biggest reasons for this shift. Yes, you have to purchase the toys and tools to set up shop at home, but it is also the cost associated with the corporate structure. Use an example of a company with one thousand employees, that is a lot of office space and cubicles to rent, which require multiple floors of space for your employees. Add in the cost associated with utilities, heat, air conditioning, electricity, and insurance. Add it up, it is cheaper for the company to set you up in an office at home. Yes, you still need to have a corporate structure but you do not need office space for one thousand employees, and it does not have to be as massive as it was before. You can still show off by saying that, "We have taken advantage of the technology that is at out finger tips. Even though it might not look like it at this corporate office, we employ over one thousand employees who are connected to us virtually from their home offices."

Some jobs are partial telecommuting jobs, where employees can split their time between the corporate office and the home office. Three days one week at home, two days in the office, or one week at home, one week in the office. This can be rotated between employees requiring less overall office space. It creates an affect similar to a hotel where you come and go. Companies that want to be "greener" with their approach can also implement telecommuting, by keeping employees at home. It means there is less physical commuting, with less cars on the road, which can potentially improve traffic flow. Companies can receive a tax break if they can show that a larger percentage of their employees are telecommuting.

This is not a knock on telecommuting but more of a knock on the world we live in today. In the traditional corporate structure, if you had an issue that you needed to resolve at work, or had to ask a coworker for some assistance, or had to have a meeting with your manager, you walked into their office and opened up a face-to-face dialogue. This has changed as a consequence of telecommuting. It is really more of an indictment of the emailing and texting mentality that we live in today. Even in the corporate structure you can be sitting right next to someone. Instead of verbalizing your message, you send a text message or email. This does make you more efficient at work, but has made all of society less verbal. This is becoming a problem especially with the younger demographic, who grew up with this technology.

The virtual worker, working from the virtual office, can possibly have to fight through potential drawbacks of their virtual existence. Telecommuters (virtual workers) are not visible to management and can be concerned that they are sequestered from co-workers and management. From the management perspective it can be problematic to develop an allegiance to the organization, and collaboration among co-workers can suffer when the workers are dispersed geographically. Brainstorming, where in the traditional corporate setting, involved being locked in a room together with other co-workers, and not let out of the room until a solution was reached, has been transformed into virtual brainstorming. This can be a concern of management that creativity can be compromised, because the swapping of ideas, and bouncing ideas off of each other, at one time was a productive, physical interaction by employees, does not exist in the virtual office. It can be accomplished to a lesser degree via the aforementioned technology, but the benefits of physical collaboration interaction and proximity are sacrificed.

SECTION 2

How to Get From Knocking on Doors to Becoming the CEO

This section details the relationship between the salesperson and the Human Resource Department and highlights such issues as the hiring process, interview process, performance reviews, and the career path that a salesperson can have.

Chapter 3

Salespeople and Human Resources: Getting the Sales Job That You Want

Two departments within the corporate structure that have exploded in size and significance are the Marketing Department and the Human Resource Department (HR). There are several components of the relationship between the Human Resource Department and the life of a salesperson that need to be addressed.

There is a pendulum of power that swings between management and the employee. A swing too far in either direction can give an unfair advantage to either side. In a bad economy, where jobs are sparse, the pendulum will swing too far towards the side of management. There are two sides to a company, employees who generate revenue for the company and employees who do not. With the advent of downsizing, where jobs are being slashed left and right, the first employees to go are the departments who do not generate revenue. Those on the sales side of the organization have always been exempt from downsizing. Without salespeople in the field, who is selling your product, and servicing your customers? There is no revenue to collect unless something gets sold. However, the current economy has been so bleak that the downsizing has spread across the organization. Even revenue generating jobs, such as salespeople, have fallen victim to the wrath of corporate downsizing.

The average cost of a salesperson including base salary, commission, bonuses, expenses, and benefits can easily approach one hundred and fifty thousand dollars, per year, per salesperson. If a company condenses, eliminates, or closes down ten territories, that can be a one million five hundred thousand dollar savings to the bottom line. You have to balance how much revenue will be compromised by eliminating ten salespeople. Unfortunately, in today's marketplace, several companies have made the decision that the revenue does not cover the expense and sales jobs are being eliminated. The result is that companies are going to battle with fewer salespeople. Territories are being eliminated. When a salesperson leaves a company, the position is not being filled. Instead the territory is being absorbed into the territories that have a geographical boundary with the now vacant territory. A consequence is that the salespeople in the neighboring territories now have inherited more geography, more customers, more quota, and border on spreading themselves too thin.

The pendulum has swung so far in the direction of management for all jobs that a, "Take it or leave it" mentality has set in. If a company decides not to give out a merit raise at the end of the year, tough luck. If you think that your quota is unrealistic and inflated, tough luck. If you are not happy with the way that you are being treated, "There's the door, try to replace the job that you have today, good luck." Too much power towards the side of management. The pendulum has never swung so far away from the employee than it has today.

Hiring Process

Finding any job, not just a sales job, has become an incredible challenge that can become frustrating, degrading, and humiliating. Who is more desperate in today's marketplace, the candidate or the company? Desperation on behalf of a candidate is not a negative, it can separate you from other candidates by twisting your desperation into a statement to the company that you really want the job. Not only are there fewer opportunities, there is an abundance of qualified candidates that make your chance of landing the job that you want even more remote. A direct result of the corporate downsizing, where territories are being consolidated, is that good salespeople do not leave good sales jobs, with good territories. In a robust job market salespeople will leave a company for a perceived better opportunity. That is not the case today. There is less job movement due to the unknown threat that you can be downsized at your new company in the near future.

The first thing to understand is that finding a sales job is a full-time job. It must start early on Monday morning and continue through Friday evening. You must exhaust all means of getting your resume in front of the hiring manager. Using the Internet, recruiters, mailing your resume directly to companies, attending job fairs, networking with former colleagues, your school's alumni association, whatever the method, you have to be proactive. A big change in Corporate America is the length of the hiring process. There was a time when you went on an interview, answered a few questions, and if the hiring manager liked what they saw they possibly could offer you a job on the spot. Those days are long gone for a few reasons. The cost to hire, recruit, and train a salesperson has skyrocketed. Most of the cost is associated with sales training. Some companies believe in training as an investment in the development of their employees. Some products that are complex require an extended training program, all contributing to the astronomical cost.

The word today is "fit", are you the right fit for the organization? A company does not want to incur the expense associated with recruiting, hiring, and training only to have the salesperson leave the organization because they were not the right fit. When this happens the entire process has to be restarted and companies are trying to avoid making the mistake of a "bad hire". What is the result? It becomes a system of checks and balances where many levels of sales management have to concur and sign off to identify the best candidate. It slows the entire process down, including several interviews taking place with multiple levels of the sales management team. You might have to interview with the District Sales Manager, the Regional Sales Manager, the Director of Sales, the Director of Sales Training, the Vice-President of Human Resources, and even the President or CEO of the company. This all takes time, and as mentioned before these interviews can be spread apart in different geographical headquarters, slowing down the process further.

Resume

Your resume is just one piece of the puzzle that helps to answer the question, "Why should I hire you?" There has been a long debate as to how long should your resume be? One page or longer? A sales resume is different from any other kind of resume. A sales resume is different because on a sales resume you should: document and itemize what you have sold, indicate what your performance was versus your unrealistic and inflated quota, state where you ranked compared to other salespeople in the company, state what milestones or promotions you earned, and any sales awards that you may have won. The more successful that you are, the longer your resume will be. If your accomplishments stretch your resume to more than one page, and possibly to multiple pages, so be it. Do not be shy. Your resume is helping you answer the management question, "Why should I hire you?"

Items can include how many years you made the quota, list the actual sales for your territory versus what your quota was, and calculate that percentage and list it. Awards such as salesperson of the month, rookie of the year, one hundred percent quota club, salesperson of the year, and President's Club Winner (an award given to the top salespeople in the company for the year). Also include promotions to field sales trainer, senior sales representative, and also special projects that you might have worked on during the year. This can include assignments such as new-product development, and participation in sales councils that meet with senior management. The more successful that you are, the more content you can add to your resume. You almost have to itemize year by year what you accomplished that year. As previously mentioned, it is rare to surpass your quota every year, so there might be some gaps between successes. The good manager will understand this, the micro-manager will not and might question you as to what happened in this year. Over time your resume should represent a body of work that does for the long haul detail success as a salesperson. (See Exhibit #2)

What if you are light on the accomplishments? Should you embellish sales statistics on your resume? Understand that over time sales managers move on to other opportunities so it may become difficult for your prospective employer to verify the statistics that you have on your resume. Many times the new company will just call into the Human Resource Department from your previous employer and ask to verify the dates of employment. With privacy laws, and in today's politically correct environment they might not want to pry into your background with your previous employer. The dates that you said you worked for a company are important, and you need to be accurate with your dates of employment. What if you have a gap in employment on your resume? Years ago this was a huge red flag that you were out of work for an extended period of time. In today's market where so many people are out of work, including so many good sales people, it has become more acceptable to have a gap in employment on your resume. An old trick was to lengthen the date when you left a company on your resume. Even though you left the company in March, you would put on your resume that you left in June. Hence, you might not start your next opportunity until September, but on your resume you state that your start date was July, eliminating the gap which realistically was from March until September.

In today's electronic, paperless environment it is also difficult to verify sales accomplishments. Electronic mail rules the day and you might be notified of winning an award or surpassing your quota via email. In the paper days you received a letter, on company letterhead, from your sales manager, national sales manager, and even from the President or CEO of your company, recognizing and thanking you for your effort and lauding your success. It was easy to save this letter and accumulate a file or stack of letters that you received over time. You would bring these with you on your interview and supplement and legitimize what you have on your resume. Today you have to print out the email and hope that it is signed with a fancy signature and title, it is just not the same thing. Most companies give out some type of hardware in the form of trophies, plaques, or watches that commemorate your achievement. Why not bring them with you, or at least have a picture of them in your office, to help you answer the question, "Why should I hire you?"

Exhibit #2 Sample Resume Listing Accomplishments

Jane Doe

123 Elm Street

Anytown, USA

Phone/Email/Fax

January 2008-Present: ABC Inc.
Salesperson
Selling entire line of ABC products.

Accomplishments:

2012	102.3% of Quota, 9th in country out of 50 Salespeople
	Member 100% Quota Club
	Territory Sales $1,023,000 vs. Quota 1,000,000
2011	Promotion to Field Sales Trainer
2010	118.0% of Quota, 2nd in country out of 50 Salespeople
	Presidents Club Winner for Sales Achievement
	Territory Sales $1,180,000 vs. Quota $1,000,000
2009	Rookie of the Year Award Winner
	Sales Person of the Month for May 2009
2008	Sales Trainee, completed formal Sales Training Program

Job Description

It is imperative to know as much about a job as possible before you make the leap and jump on the ship. Once you are on the ship it is not easy to jump off, and once you jump off the ship you are on your own. Make sure you know what you are getting involved in before you accept the offer. A job description is a listing of duties and activities that details the daily activities and expectations of a job. It is your responsibility to have a thorough understanding of what you are getting involved in. Once you accept a job offer it is difficult to go back to the job that you just left, so you better be sure that this is the correct decision that you have made.

There are a few safeguards that can act as signals if this is the right opportunity for you. The first question to ask is directed to hit your potential sales manager right between the eyes. "What is it like to work for you?" That is a great question, and you want to know up front what you are getting involved in, and what their expectations are. Follow-up inquiries such as what is a typical day like, a typical week, a typical month? Sales managers can put you in touch with other salespeople that work for them, that might be a little more forthcoming with the truth. A smart idea is to do some homework on your own and talk to customers who are currently using your prospective new product. Talk to customers who do not, and use your potential competitor's product, ask them why they chose the product that they use. Customers can provide a wealth of information. The most reliable way to see if an opportunity is for you is to spend time, live, in the field with a salesperson who currently is selling the product. This benefits both sides. During an interview a picture can be painted about an opportunity that looks attractive, but until you are in a live selling situation you really don't know. You might accept a job offer and you think you have a great product to sell only to find that the market prefers your competitor's.

Customers are funny, either they are looking for the best quality product and sometimes do not mind paying a premium price for quality, or they are looking for the cheapest way to solve their problem. Being on either side of the price versus quality spectrum is not undesirable because some customers are looking for one or the other. What if your product is in the middle, it is not the best one, and it is not the cheapest alternative, so you are stuck in the middle, which can put you in a tough selling situation. How do you know this when you are thinking about accepting a position? Many products are being commoditized and it is becoming difficult to differentiate the features and benefits between product alternatives. This has forged a "me too" environment, where a salesperson's response to a customer objection is, "My product can do that too!" In the case of too many alternatives and not enough differentiation among alternatives, service can be what makes a difference. If your selling style is rooted in serving the customer, then this can become an attractive opportunity.

Spending time in the field with a salesperson, or doing your customer homework on your own, can resolve this question. When you travel with a salesperson ask yourself: How are they received by their customers? Are they welcomed? Are the customers happy to see them? Do they make complimentary remarks about the salesperson, company, and product in front of you? If they do not, and they lodge complaints about the company or product, or are very curt with their comments, this can be a message to watch what you get involved with. The more time that you can spend in the field with a salesperson the better. Remember, they have the same job that you are interviewing for, if you get a thorough understanding of what their job is like on a daily basis, it can clear the clouds of indecision in your mind about moving forward and accepting the opportunity.

Job Interview

The notion that you only get one chance to make a first impression cannot be more true about getting a job today, especially a sales job. The second that you walk in the door the hiring manager is making a judgment about you, and you can blow it from the time you walk in the door until the time you introduce yourself, shake their hand and sit down. How long does that take, twenty seconds? Instantaneous judgments made by sales managers can be about how you approach them, how you introduce yourself, how you shake their hand, what you are wearing, and a sense of how you carry yourself. Do you come across as confident and professional, or do you come across as arrogant or too shy? An interview for a sales job is different than any other job. The first thing that you are selling is yourself on any job interview, but if you do a poor job of selling yourself, how can a sales manager expect you to do a good job of selling the company's product?

You need to look for clues about how you are doing during the interview. The best sales managers take your resume put it to the side, look you in the eye, and ask you to tell them something about yourself and why you are the right person for this position. The micro-managing sales manager goes to the bottom of your resume and interrogates you line by line about why you left one job for another, and ask you why they should hire you? Keep in mind that they have already read your resume, they had to. There is something on your resume that has caught their eye, which compelled them to call you in for an interview.

A long-standing technique that sales managers practice during an interview that is designed to measure your sales ability on the spot is the, "sell me this pen," scenario. In the middle of the interview, unannounced, with no chance of you preparing, the sales manager will whip out a pen, place it in front of you on the desk and say, "sell me this pen." It can be uncomfortable and is designed to be uncomfortable. What they are looking for is your ability to spot a feature of a product and come up with a benefit as to why the customer should purchase the product. It is a selling technique called, "feature/benefit selling", where you point out the characteristics (features) of a product, and explain why (benefit) this product is the solution that you are looking for.

A way for you to counter the "sell me this pen" scenario is to bring a sample of the product that you have been selling with you to the interview. After you sell the sales manager the pen, show them how you sell your product. Place your product in their hands and point out the features and benefits of your product. This can go a long way during the interview by showing your ability to practice "feature/benefit selling" by the way that you demonstrate how you currently sell your product.

Technology has inched its way into the interview process. Telephone interviews have always been a part of the interview process, especially early on in the process, often as a method of screening candidates. It is a cost effective way to screen initial candidates. A hiring manager can make the call from their office. There is no need for face-to-face interviews which can incur the expense of travel to and from the interview location for both the candidate and the company. Cell phone technology gets better every day, but conducting a phone interview on a cell or smart phone can be risky. The quality of the call, background noise, and the possibility of the call being lost are all issues that need to be considered. You are better off on a land line phone in your office, with no background distractions. You need to be prepared, watch what you say and how you say it. The same rule about a first impression applies and you can be at a disadvantage over the phone. You cannot impress them with your physical appearance over the phone. There is no question that the phone interview will be replaced by the virtual interview, where they will be able to see you through a webcam or other device. The same rules apply as if this was a physical interview. Dress for success, as opposed to not dressing for success. Not doing so because you are not physically in front of them, can cost you the opportunity of moving to the next step in the interview process.

The use of Powerpoint has crept into the interview process. It is a great idea to prepare a short Powerpoint presentation, no more than ten slides, that can highlight your accomplishments. This can give you the opportunity to show what you know about your products, market, industry and competition. An outstanding idea is to download a copy of the logo of the company who you are interviewing with, and make that the first page of your presentation with your name and date of the interview at the bottom. You can bring hard copies of your presentation with you to the interview, to supplement your resume and letters of recommendation and awards. Then email a copy of the presentation before the interview, bring your laptop with you and play the presentation during the interview. This can separate you from the other candidates and demonstrate how interested you are in the opportunity.

The bigger the company, the more corporate they are, and the more politically correct they are. Some companies will ask the exact same questions to every candidate. You can spot this by how general a question is, compared to a question that is more tailored to your background. You have to be careful how you answer these questions, you cannot be confrontational because you feel that this is an inappropriate question to ask. Remember they are searching for responses that eliminate your candidacy, so sit there, think about what you are going to say, and try to be as positive as you can be with your response.

There are too many qualified candidates for one sales job today. Hiring managers are looking for ways to disqualify candidates from the process. The best way is by the questions that they pose during an interview. "What do you know about our company, What can you tell me about our products, What do you know about our industry and competition?" If you sit there with a blank stare and no response because you have not done your homework, they are going to say, "next", and you will be disqualified. All of this information is at your fingertips. Go to the Internet, locate their website, and download every page that is possible. Hiring managers love it when a candidate walks into an interview with this information in their hands, especially information on their company's history. If you are prepared you will be able to answer these questions. That will show the hiring manager that you took the initiative to do your due diligence on the opportunity, and that alone can separate you from the other candidates.

Interview questions can be a sore spot, but the way that you answer the questions can make or break how successful or how disastrous the interview went. The reason for the trepidation about the interview questions is that you have to answer the question. The questions are so vague that you do not know what answer the sales manager is looking for. If you could read their mind and answer the question with a response that they are looking for, you would do that. You cannot read their mind, so your anxiety level rises when a question is posed to you and you are not sure how to answer it. Interview questions are designed to rattle you, to shake you up, to see how you respond under pressure, and this can be extremely uncomfortable. Especially if this is the job opportunity of your life and you do not want to blow it in twenty seconds with a response that the sales manager is not looking for.

Some of the most uncomfortable questions are, "Why should I hire you? Tell me about your strengths and weaknesses? Where do you want to be in five years?" All brutal, unfair questions that you have to be prepared to answer. Your response to the question, "Why should I hire you?" can be, "I am the right fit for your organization" then recite what you have done in the past that makes you the right fit for an organization, "fit" is a trendy word. On both ends of the hiring and firing process, "The candidate is a great fit for what we are looking for in the position." Consequently, "The candidate just was not the right fit for our organizational structure." Strengths and weaknesses is a harsh question to ask as well. What do you do? You cannot come across too boldly by proclaiming that you are a super hero with only strengths and no weaknesses. You cannot itemize character flaws that you might have either. The proper response is directly list a weakness but twist the meaning around to indirectly make it sound like a strength. For example, many companies have implemented work-life balance programs, where they want you to have a life outside of work because it can relieve stress and lead to a happy, enriched, and fulfilled employee. Components of these programs include the encouragement of spending quality time with your family. Your response to the weakness question can be, "I find myself getting so wrapped up in my work, that I am not spending enough quality time with my family." This acknowledges the weakness, but the indirect message is that you enjoy your work, you are a perfectionist, and are willing to give up quality time with your family to complete a task.

Where do you want to be in five years is the trickiest of all interview questions. It is difficult to answer because the answer to this one lies within the soul of the individual sales manager. Some want one answer and some want the polar opposite answer. Their feeling about this response can absolutely separate the micro-managing sales manager from the great sales manager. There are two directions that your response can go in. The first one, "I want to be a sales manager in five years." The micro-manager absorbs the response, looks at you and your resume and believes that you are a great candidate for this job. You exude tremendous potential, so much potential that you can possibly replace them as a sales manager down the road, so you just blew it with that response.

The other end of the spectrum is the sales manager who is jumping out of their seat with the exact same response. Remember, as a sales manager you are only as good as the sales people who you hire and deploy into the field. A salesperson who has the drive and determination to succeed, which can eventually get them promoted into sales management, is someone who you want on your team because they will do whatever it takes to surpass their quota. Why this is appealing to the sales manager, is that if all of their salespeople have this drive and determination, their team will exceed their quota, and the sales manager will make their quota. The end result is that they can get promoted to a senior sales management position, opening up the slot that they have been occupying.

Other questions that can be uncomfortable during an interview are questions related to why did you leave you previous employer? Do you tell the truth? What if your sales manager micro-managed you every day, or what if the quota that was in place was inflated and unrealistic? What do you say? The first thing to say is that it was a fine company to work for. Never talk negatively about a previous employer because that might be the way that you feel about your new employer and that is not good. Never burn a bridge. While you may think that you work in a huge industry, you never know who you will turn up in the future. You could end up working for someone from your previous employer down the road. A good answer is to always tie it into compensation and you are looking for a better financial opportunity. Sales managers want to hire salespeople who want to maximize their earning potential, and while you had a positive experience at your last company, you were not able to reach the financial goals that you are looking for.

A legitimate and superb question for a candidate for a sales position to ask is, "If this is such a great opportunity, what happened to the last salesperson who had this job?" Job opportunities today are few and far between, especially good to great job opportunities. Forever, salespeople who were not happy with their current situation would leave a job to pursue a more attractive opportunity. Promotional opportunities might be available by leaving your company and accepting a promotion, but you need to leave you current company to accept the promotion. This created movement and mobility for salespeople. The current economic atmosphere has stunted this growth. Factor in the shrinking of sales forces and the specter of looming downsizing has forced many salespeople to sit tight and be forced to be happy with their current situation. So there is not as much movement and not as many openings. When an opening does come up and if it is a great opportunity, which is rare, it begs the following question, "If this is such a great opportunity, why is it available." Good salespeople do not leave great territories. Something maybe wrong with the picture, it could be a great opportunity with a crummy territory.

There are acceptable, genuine reasons why an attractive territory may become available. Maybe the previous salesperson did such an outstanding job that they accepted a promotion into sales management, creating the vacancy, or maybe it is an expansion territory. The prior salesperson relocated to another part of the country, left to start a family, or unfortunately passed away (possibly from the stress associated with the inflated quota). There are equally unacceptable excuses as to why the territory is open including, it was a bad hire, not the right fit, or it just did not work out.

Interview time can also be a clue, sometimes you are told up front that you have a certain amount of time for the interview, for example sixty minutes. If the sales manager ends the interview abruptly, or before the allotted time, barring an emergency that has just come up, is not a good sign about how you did during the interview. Hence, if the interview is going smoothly and all of a sudden you realize that you have gone past the allotted time of sixty minutes, can be a signal that you are doing well. You have to have a sense when you have taken up enough of their time and do not want to drag the interview or start to waste the sales manager's time. The biggest difference between a sales job interview and any other is how do you end the interview. In a sales job interview you must close the sales manager the same way that you would close a sale. You must ask for the order or in this case ask for the job.

There are softer, more professional ways than others to ask for the job. The first comment that you must make is to always thank them for taking the time out of their busy schedule to meet with you. Then you need to express your interest in the opportunity. Some suggestions can be, "Have I answered all of your questions or concerns about my background? If so I would like to take the next steps, and what would the next steps be?" They can respond with, "I am interviewing several candidates today and I will be reviewing the candidates with my boss?" You need to respond with, "Can I schedule a second interview with you or your boss, I am available next Tuesday or Thursday?"

You need to push for the second interview. The mentality from sales management is that if you do not push them to take the next steps, and push for a follow-up meeting, how can they expect that you will do this when you are in front of a customer who needs to be pushed or prodded along to get to the next step of the sales process?

Performance Review

Most companies will put you through some type of performance review process where they will sit down with you and review your performance for the year. Some choose to do this annually, semi-annually, or quarterly. To be up front and honest, this is an uncomfortable exercise on both sides, but get used to it. Get used to being knocked down and criticized for even the smallest, most insignificant issues. This is a corporate tool designed to knock you off of your pedestal, humiliate you, and remind you who is the boss.

The best example is how major league baseball treats their players (employees) during the arbitration process. Arbitration in baseball is a legal battle in court where both sides present their case, in front of a mediator. This process is all about salary negotiation. The player, actually through the voice of their agent, itemizes their statistical performance that can justify the salary increase that they are looking for. How many home runs did they hit, their batting average, how many runs did they drive in, how many runs did they score, and how many game winning hits did they have that led to team victories? All legitimate, positive statistics to help support the request for the salary increase. The team counters with negative statistics designed to drive the salary price down. Statistics such as how many times did you strike out, how many runners did you leave in scoring position, how many errors you made in the field, and how many times did you get thrown out trying to steal a base? The mediator listens to both sides and then makes a decision that is binding, meaning that both sides agree to the decision with no appeal process.

The difference with being the salesperson compared to being the baseball player is that you do not get to plead your case in front of a mediator. Unfortunately, your sales manager and company are judge, jury, and executioner in this case and you have to throw yourself on the mercy of the court. The decision is binding, meaning that you do not have any recourse but to live with their decision, again if you do not like it, "There is the door!"

It is easier to measure your performance in a sales job compared to other corporate jobs because your performance is evaluated by a number, did you make the quota assigned to you or not? It is easy to quantify. Comparing this to the baseball analogy, you support your case by stating how many new accounts you opened, what specific projects you worked on this year, and what your sales were versus the quota. Your sales manager will counter with how many times your expense reports went over budget or were not delivered on time. How many times your sales call reports were late, and how inaccurate your sales forecasts were. You might have made the unrealistic, inflated quota overall, but you only exceeded the quota for three of the five products that the company was promoting for the year. Digest that one!

Some type of numerical scale is put in place to evaluate your performance, in this example a scale of one to five, with one being unacceptable and five being over achieving. The first thing to get in your mind and heart is that you will never achieve a five or whatever is deemed the highest number, and this is so wrong, and a flaw in the process. The top number is unattainable and they keep it that way as a carrot for you to chase. If it is unattainable then why is it on the scale? You can break all kinds of records for sale achievement, including shattering records of previous salespeople, but you will never get the five out of five. It is designed that way to keep pushing you and it is a carrot that you will never catch. What is the purpose of a scale from one to five, if five is unattainable? Make the scale one to four. If your company does that, then a score of four will never be attainable. This is a battle that you will never win, so get used to it and take your medicine.

Attitude Versus Performance

Sales is a numbers driven life and you are only as good as you last sale. What gets lost in the shuffle is your attitude, compared to your performance. From the first day that you walk into an organization, regardless if you are a salesperson on the revenue side of the organization or not, management is looking to place a label on you. Once this label is established, in a positive or negative way, it is an indelible imprint that is almost impossible to change. It is a tattoo that is placed on your forehead. Labels can include "good potential", "possible management candidate", and other labels can be placed on you that are not as favorable.

Spending your life in the field means that you are not exposed to, and you do not have the opportunity to interact with senior management on a daily basis. Your interaction will be monitored at corporate functions such as national sales meetings, corporate sales training exercises, and trade shows. When you do get the opportunity to interact with senior management, your attitude can make or break you. You can be at the top of the charts when it comes to sales quota achievement, even on a consistent basis, and not a one year wonder. If you waste your five minutes of time in front of senior sales management venting your displeasure with the unattainable, inflated quota, or with problems that are product related, or any other complaints associated with your life as a salesperson, you will get the label of a malcontent tattooed on your forehead. Senior sales management knows what the issues are and you do not have to echo them. As opposed to the average salesperson, and in average it means making the quota, missing the quota, but certainly not the superstar salesperson who consistently surpasses the quota. If that salesperson gets the ear of senior sales management and emphasizes how much they love their job, their products, and their company. Positive,

positive, positive compared to the negative. Who do you think makes a better impression? Understand that the superstar salesperson will eventually succumb to the unrealistic and inflated quota and then what are you left with? Bad performance and bad attitude. When someone needs to get promoted who is in a more favorable position? Attitude can and will trump performance every time.

Expenses

How a company pays the out of pocket field expenses to a salesperson can be a signal or a clue about how the company treats and regards its salespeople. Of course there are exceptions to every rule, but when you have to make the decision to join one company over another and you do not have sufficient background information as to which is the correct opportunity to pursue, expenses can tell a lot. Some companies reimburse every dime of out of pocket expenses. For some sales jobs, the salesperson incurs all expenses, while others are in the middle, where they will reimburse for some expenses and not others.

How much out of pocket expenses can a sales person incur? The average sales territory can incur annual expenses that exceed twenty thousand to thirty thousand dollars a year in expenses. The more travel, the more expense, and that number can exceed thirty thousand dollars quickly. Start adding it up:

Auto:

Car payment, car insurance, gasoline, tolls, parking, maintenance, repairs, rental car when your car is being serviced/repaired, car wash

Home Office:

Smart/cell phone, internet charges: home office and wireless charges while in the field, office phone, laptop computer, tablet, printer/fax/scanner, printer paper, copies, office supplies, postage/shipping charges

Travel:

Airfare, transportation to and from airport, hotel, meals while traveling

Miscellaneous:

Entertainment of customers, samples, tuition reimbursement

The more of the items listed above that are reimbursed the better the company. There are jobs where the salesperson literally does not spend any of their money on out of pocket expenses. Another message is how long does it take to receive the reimbursement from your company. Some companies take advantage of the software and spread sheet technology and can reimburse expenses into your bank account through direct deposit within a week of submission of the expense report. Some companies take their time and complete expense reimbursement once a month. The more expedient, the better. Remember, in most cases the salesperson has to incur the expense and then is reimbursed. It is your money, if you delay the submission of your expense report, this will delay the reimbursement. When you consider the amount of expense that can be incurred, it is the responsibility of the salesperson to submit the expense report as soon as possible.

Some companies will issue corporate credit cards, or gasoline cards, which have their advantages and disadvantages. An advantage to the salesperson is that some expenses can be directly billed to your company credit card and there is less of a capital outlay by the salesperson. An advantage to the company is that it can provide a neat, and organized monthly statement that can make it easier to manage expenses. A disadvantage to the salesperson is that the company issued card can become a tool for management to track your activity, when you bought gasoline, where you bought gasoline, also did you buy gasoline on the weekend, or outside of your geographical territory?

Why does a company give a salesperson a company car? Is it because they want to be nice to their salespeople? They will make you think so, but this is not the motive. A company car, where the salesperson incurs zero out of pocket expense (Except minor IRS tax charges), is issued because it eliminates all excuses of why you should be in the field. Excuses like, "My car broke down, I have a flat tire, I cannot afford the gasoline, my insurance ran out," are all eliminated. Even when your company car is in for repair or service is not an excuse, your company will set you up with a rental vehicle eliminating the excuse of, "I cannot go and make sales calls because I do not have my car."

You are not going to be issued a luxury car, but you are not going to be issued a compact car either. The average company car is a mid-sized sedan that today can range in the twenty-five to thirty-five thousand dollar range. Some companies will provide you a larger vehicle including some that will provide you with a sport utility vehicle. There is another message with this one. They are not providing you with a sport utility vehicle so your kids can be comfortable in the company car, they are giving you the sport utility vehicle because you will either be lugging large pieces of capital equipment in and out of the car for presentations, or it is filled with samples or brochures that you need on you sales calls. This expense absolutely is considered compensation and should be factored into your decision about whether to join a company or not.

If you have a job where you entertain customers on a regular basis, can be another reason why the company car is provided. So much of sales and marketing is image. A company wants to portray a professional image to their customers and a company car can enhance this image. Most companies do allow for personal use of the car for you and possibly your spouse, children are typically excluded. A tip is to fill up your company car with gasoline during the week, frequent weekend fill ups are a red flag that you are using your company car more for pleasure than for business. This is the best situation to have for one specific reason. When you have the company car it is one less detail that you have to worry about. How you get to and from work, and how you get from customer to customer is taken off of the table.

Most companies have eliminated the use of company cars. It is not because they do not want to be nice to their salespeople, but for one reason and one reason only, liability. A company car is covered under the company's insurance policy and if you are in a car accident, the company can be sued. Today it is fashionable to have a car allowance program put in place. A car allowance is a lump sum of money paid to the salesperson on a monthly basis to cover the cost of a car payment and car insurance. Alternative car allowance plans pay a flat price per mile that is driven. Advantages are that you get to pick the kind of car that you want to drive every day, as opposed to the company providing you with a car that you might not be fond of. The disadvantage is that the car allowance is taxed as income, so the amount that you receive for your car allowance, is not what you get every month to make your car payment and pay your car insurance, so it brings you back into the ball park of the mid-sized sedan. Company cars are taxed, but it is very low and tied into how many personal miles you have driven, and not the same as a car allowance.

The biggest fundamental difference between the company car, and car allowance, is that under the car allowance program, it is your car, and you are responsible for all maintenance and repairs. Yes, this is factored into your car allowance, but once you exhaust your car allowance you are paying out of your own pocket. Understand this, you live in your car as a salesperson and your car will take a physical beating just from the wear and tear that you put on it, not only from the amount of miles that you log, but from the starts and stops of frequent sales calls made during the day. If you purchase your car new, after three years your car will have much more mileage and wear and tear than the average car. If you lease your car and use your car allowance to make your lease payments, you will exceed your mileage allotment and have other issues to deal with at the end of the lease.

Most company cars are turned over every two to three years, under this plan you would receive a new car every few years, this is tied into how many miles you drive, so you will not have the issues associated with the car allowance plan.

Some sales jobs require more overnight travel than others. Size and geography of your territory will dictate how much overnight travel you will do. How does your company handle overnight travel expenses? This is another message that can tell you what kind of company you work for. Some companies believe that if you are on the road and away from your family you should have the option to stay wherever you are most comfortable and safe regardless of price. This has to be handled within reason, you do not need to stay at the most expensive hotel in town, you should use your judgment, but you also want to be close to your first sales call. If a cheaper hotel is an hour away from your first sales call, you might want to weigh the alternatives. Some companies do not care that you are on the road, consider it part of your job, and will only reimburse for the cheapest hotel, regardless of location, safety, or comfort. Some companies have corporate travel departments that book the reservation for you and will look for the least expensive hotel choice, remember they are not staying there!

How are meals while traveling handled? Most companies will provide a per diem, or per day meal allowance. Some are meager, which only allow for a cup of coffee and a piece of toast for breakfast, a slice of pizza and a soda for lunch, and a small allowance for a dinner entrée. Some are more generous than others. Now you are not going to have filet mignon and lobster tails, served with an expensive bottle of wine (unless you are entertaining customers), but a fair meal plan is somewhere between a piece of toast and a lobster tail.

The same applies for airfare, where depending on the job, especially sales management, who spend more time flying than salespeople in the field. Flying first class is rare and is usually only possible with upgrades from previous travel. Do you fly non-stop or not? Again many of these reservations are booked by a corporate travel office. They do not care about layovers in airports, because they are not the one traveling on business. A perquisite of excessive hotel and air travel is that you can accumulate frequent flyer miles and hotel points to earn a free vacation for your family during the year. If you are told that a perk of this job is that you will earn a free vacation, this is a message that, "You will spend so much time on this job traveling, and so much time away from your family, that you will accumulate enough points to go wherever you want," might not be something that is as enticing as it sounds.

A few final notes on expenses. Companies, even with the most liberal and creative expense accounts, including the company car policy, where there are no out of pocket expenses, will not reimburse for vehicle violations including parking tickets, and moving violations such as red light and speeding citations. It is not worth the risk to abuse your expense account. Padding your expenses with entertainment, parking, office supplies, or other miscellaneous receipts are grounds for immediate dismissal. It is not worth the risk of losing a great sales job for the opportunity to make up a few bucks on the submission of inaccurate expense reports. One of the first reports that sales management will look through with a fine tooth comb are the expense reports that you submit for reimbursement. You do need to incur expenses every month. This might sound strange but your company will look at what your expenses are in a positive way. A busy salesperson who is consistently on the road making sales calls and incurring expense is making an effort to be productive. A salesperson who spends less money on travel and entertainment of their customers can be viewed as lazy or complacent. The trick is to spend just under what you have been budgeted, submit timely expense reports, and this will never become an issue with your sales manager.

Chapter 4

Career Path: You Would Be Amazed Where a Career in Sales Can Lead You

A career in sales can offer a salesperson more opportunity to advance within a company than people realize. Starting with a company in the sales department can provide a solid foundation that may present you with several different upward mobility career paths that can lead you all the way up the corporate ladder to CEO. For many years the profile for senior management within Corporate America was that a CEO should have a financial background, and have the ability to manage and deliver a profitable bottom line. No one is suggesting that not having a bottom line mentality is important, but there are other strategies that can get you there. Today it is common for companies to have a sales and marketing vision and direction. Companies are more sales oriented, and believe that sales is what drives a business. Nothing happens until something is sold. There is no money to collect unless a sale is made. This type of mentality is a healthy way to run an organization and is increasing in popularity.

Here is an example of where the employee from the sales side of the organization can have an advantage over the employee from the financial or accounting side of the company. Both employees start their career on the same day, both have similar backgrounds and experience. There is not a lot of differentiation between the two employees except the departments where they will be working in. Five years later someone needs to be promoted into corporate management. Both candidates are asked to interview for the management position. They are asked to respond to the same questions, look at the advantage that the salesperson has over the accountant. Who would you promote?

Tell me something about our company's product? The accountant responds with, "Our product has a profit margin of thirteen percent." The salesperson responds with, "Our product can do this for a customer, and here is how it functions, and this is what it is made of, and this is how it helps customers, and these are the competitive advantages that it has over our competition."

Tell me something about our customers? The accountant responds with, "The average time it takes our customers to pay their bill is forty-five days." The salesperson responds with, "We have very demanding but loyal customers who require a tremendous amount of service and follow-up." "Our product can be very complex to operate so we need to constantly train the customer to insure that they are using our products properly. This follow-up helps us to establish a relationship with our customers which leads to brand loyalty and residual sales."

Tell me something about our competition? The accountant responds with, "Our competition has twenty-six percent market share." The salesperson with responds with, "Our competitor has a price competitive advantage, or a quality competitive advantage. Their product functions differently than ours, theirs is made of this while ours is made of something else. Our competitive advantage is that our product can do this while theirs is not able to."

Tell me something about the industry that we compete in. The accountant responds with, "Our industry is growing at an average of eleven percent per year for the past five years." The salesperson responds with, "Our industry is facing several challenges for the future. It is becoming popular for customers in our industry to look to the global marketplace for product substitutes. Government regulations are threatening to change our industry. Customers are merging together forming purchasing groups that are forcing the price of our product down."

Based on the responses, who has the best chance to get promoted and move up the ladder? This is not an indictment on the financial and accounting side of the company, but the sales side of the company has significant advantages because of the nature of their job description. The accountant sits behind a desk all day, in an office or cubicle, and is sheltered from the reality of being in the field. They only see the numbers, they do not know the reasons behind the numbers. They can tell you that we are profitable as a company but they cannot tell you why. A salesperson can tell you why because their hands are all over the product all day every day. A salesperson is on the front line and is the first line of contact for the customer. The salesperson encounters their competition consistently and lives in the field within their industry. Customers are a tremendous resource and have a wealth of information when it comes to what trends are affecting their industry, and what new products your competitors are coming out with. Salespeople live with them every day providing the exposure that allows them to answer the aforementioned questions when it comes down to who should get promoted into management.

Table #1 Career Path

CAREER SALESPERSON	SALES MANAGEMENT	HEADQUARTERS MARKETING
Sales Trainee	District Manager	Marketing Trainee
Sales Representative	Division Sales Manager	Assistant Product Manager
Senior Sales Representative	Regional Sales Manager	Associate Product Manager
Field Sales Trainer	Area/Zone Sales Manager	Senior Product Manager
Career Salesperson	Director of Sales (National Sales Manager)	Director of Marketing
	Vice-President of Sales	Vice-President of Marketing
	CEO/President	CEO/President

Three career paths (See Table #1) will be discussed all providing options that can best suit your dreams, aspirations, and lifestyle: career salesperson, sales management, and headquarters marketing. Typically you will find that advantages of one career path can be disadvantages of the other paths. There is a hidden beauty in choosing a career in sales that goes unnoticed. Sales and marketing departments are exploding with the shift towards a more sales driven company than an accounting and finance driven company. Opportunities are endless with most people not realizing that all of these positions within a company can be achieved all by starting out in the sales department. The biggest challenge today is getting your foot in the door with a company giving you an entry-level job. The easiest way to get your foot in the door is as a salesperson selling the company's product.

Career Salesperson

The career salesperson career path starts with entering the company as a sales trainee. Depending on the company's commitment and complexity of the product line will determine how long you remain as a trainee. Once you graduate from the sales training program you are now out in the field starting your career as a salesperson selling your company's product. You spend a few years establishing your territory, demonstrate some success, surpass your quota more often than not and you are promoted to Senior Sales Representative. Nothing changes in your daily day-to-day job activity, you are just recognized by management for what you have achieved. You may receive an increase in your base salary or a bonus. The point of this promotion is to reward you, and begin to separate the salespeople who have surpassed their quota, compared to the other salespeople who may be struggling. Over time there can be different levels of senior representative status, senior representative one, two, three or bronze, silver, gold, and platinum to distinguish the senior representatives among each other.

At some point you may be asked to accept a promotion to become part of the sales training team as a Field Sales Trainer. Your day-to-day job as a sales representative remains the same except that now you may be asked to train the new salespeople who enter the organization. This is an assignment that you should accept for one reason. Sales management is sending an indirect message to you by promoting you to Field Sales Trainer. The message is that we like you, and want to groom, and earmark you as a potential candidate for sales management down the road. They are happy with your performance, your style of selling, and the way that you represent the company. They want you to train the company's new salespeople. You can receive another increase in base salary, plus a stipend for every salesperson that you train. Most companies utilize multiple sales training formats that will be detailed in other chapters, including classroom training, vestibule training, which creates a sales situation in a simulated environment, and field sales training. Your role will be to have the sales trainee shadow you in the field and ride shotgun with you in your car for a period of time to see what the actual day-to-day situations are that you encounter in the field on a daily basis. The difference between the field sales training compared to the classroom and vestibule formats is that you are live in the field and nothing can recreate a live selling situation.

At this point, to reach Senior Sales Representative and Field Sales Trainer status can take some time to climb these steps. There will then come a time when sales management will ask you about your career aspirations and possibly offer you a promotion into sales management or headquarters marketing. This is your opportunity to cross-over into another side of the company and can be a major fork in the road for you and your future. Some salespeople get tired of the grind associated with being in the field and are looking for a new challenge. Some salespeople realize that, while they like their company and their products, sales might not be the right long-term destination for them, but advertising, or public relations for the company might be, so they can move into headquarters marketing. Some salespeople want to make the leap into sales management, which keeps you on the sales side of the company but presents different challenges that will be addressed. What if you love the life of a career salesperson? What if you enjoy the freedom and independence associated with a life in the field? Understand that as soon as you make that leap towards sales management or headquarters marketing you are giving up a significant piece of the freedom and independence that you enjoy being a career salesperson.

What if you are a great salesperson and enjoy the lifestyle and want to continue the pay for performance lifestyle? Understand the best salespeople make more money than sales managers or headquarters marketing executives. It is similar to professional sports, who makes more money, the star players or the coach? A star salesperson can earn more compensation than their sales manager. So what do you do? As mentioned previously it is so important in life to find that passion and love what you do. If you love being a career salesperson there is no guarantee that you will feel the same way about sales management and headquarters marketing. You can turn down the promotion because you want to remain in the field. Promotional opportunities do not come around every day. Management will respect this decision, but understand the next opportunity for promotion can be years away. The opportunity might come around again, and maybe your aspirations have changed and you make the leap, but if you turn down that promotion a second time there might not be a third. Companies look to place labels on employees all of the time, "This one has potential for management, this one does not." If you turn down that promotion a second time you can be labeled a Career Sales Person. This is not a negative but management looks at your profile and put you in the pile of employees who are happy with their existence and position within this organization, but will never move up the corporate ladder.

This is not a negative! If you love the life of being in the field and enjoy the freedom and independence, you can have a tremendous life. There is stress associated with each career path, in the field you have the stress associated with quota and customer issues, but the other two career paths offer different and possibly more severe levels of stress. If you are a great salesperson, working for a great company, with great products that you can become a master at selling, the career salesperson career path can be a great one and can last your entire work life.

Sales Management

Most people, including salespeople and sales managers, think that there is a seamless transition from moving up from salesperson to sales manager. A salesperson is a lone wolf who thinks like an individual, a sales manager is a mother hen who has to run a hen house. There are similarities between the two roles in the organization but make no mistake about it, it is a whole different ballgame. A perfect analogy is the relationship between a player and a coach in sports. How come most great players in sports are not successful as coaches or managers? Yes, there are a few exceptions but for the most part it does not work. It does not work for a few reasons. To become great at anything you have to possess the unique combination of talent and work ethic that elevates your performance above your teammates, peers, and competitors. You can possess the talent, but without the work ethic your talent will only take you so far. Consequently, without the talent you will only reach a certain level of success. The great player who becomes the coach has a hard time accepting the deficiencies of their players, who may be good but not great. The great player who now becomes the coach can struggle with the deficiencies of their players and wonder why the players cannot perform the way that they themselves performed. The same goes for the great salesperson, because of their success, and their ability to surpass the company's quota, gets the opportunity to be promoted into sales management. The great salesperson is now in place as a sales manager and has to deal with salespeople who may not be as talented, or work as hard as they did when they were a salesperson and now they are part of their team.

The analogy of sales manager to coach in sports also shares other striking similarities. A coach is only as good as the players that they put into play. Any coach who is worth their salt will tell you that you cannot win without the right players, and those who deny this are fooling themselves. It is the same with sales management. You are only as good as the salespeople that you hire and deploy into the field. Quota does not disappear because you get promoted to sales manager. In fact you have less control over the outcome of your performance because your quota as a sales manager is the sum of the sales quota achievement of your salespeople. If you assemble a great team who surpasses their quota as a group, you surpass your quota as a sales manager. If you have an average team your team will produce average results. If you have a great team your team can achieve great results.

Often you will find sales managers who will accept mediocre performance because that is not a threat to their existence as a sales manager. Why would you do this? It is done because often you have the star salespeople staying in the role of career salesperson, for the aforementioned reasons, and someone has to get promoted. Often it is the mediocre salesperson who manages to exist within the organization who realizes that they are not a great salesperson. They may want to move on and accept the promotion into sales management. Average and mediocre salespeople are hired because the star salesperson can threaten the sales manager. It happens all the time in sports where the stars run the team, the same can apply to a sales manager. Why would you not want the best possible salespeople on your team? If you recruit, hire, and develop a team of stars they will surpass their quota and you will surpass your quota as well. You can then get promoted to a higher level of sales management as a result of the team that you have put in place.

A career in sales management is a hybrid between the freedom and independence afforded to the career salesperson and the nine to five corporate existence of the career in headquarters marketing. You still have contact with customers, but you are not on the front line. You do get involved in selling activities but not to the extent of the career salesperson. It is similar to the role of a grandparent, you get to visit with your grandchildren (customers), but get to leave and shoulder the daily responsibility on the parents (salesperson).

Besides managing the personalities of your sales team a major concern about making the transition from salesperson to sales manager is travel. A career salesperson is paid to sell and a sales manager is paid to travel. Career sales people will travel to the previously mentioned corporate events during the sales year, and with the expansion of many geographical territories career salespeople can spend some time on the road. Nothing compares to the amount of time on the road that sales managers spend. A sales manager just has a larger geographical territory than the salesperson, which forces them to spend more time on the road and less time in their office. How much time on the road? Conservatively speaking, on a regular week with no sales meetings or trade shows to attend, a sales manager can spend Monday in their office and hit the road Tuesday morning. Spend three days in the field working with a salesperson from Tuesday through Thursday evening, then traveling home back to their office on Friday. That's two nights a week on the road, every week. Some weeks there can be more of a distance between the salesperson and the sales manager's home, stretching it to three nights a week. Add up the corporate sales meetings, sales training exercises, trade shows, and weekly travel with your salespeople, and you are looking at well over one hundred nights a year on the road in a hotel away from your family. The good companies will provide you with reasonable accommodations, and a meal allowance, but after a while, year after year, this can wear on you.

The size of the organization will determine how many sales managers you need. Larger organizations have more levels of management including district, division, regional, area/zone, and a national sales manager. Every company uses different vernacular to give different titles to different sales managers, these are a few examples. Span of control refers to how many subordinates report to a manager. The optimal span of control for a sales manager is seven to nine salespeople depending on how long the sales process is, how much customer interaction is required by salespeople, and how dispersed the customers are geographically. A wide span of control (more than nine) can spread a sales manager too thin, where they will not be able to provide the amount of support that they need to their salespeople. A narrow span of control (less than seven) can create a micro-management situation where a manager has too much time on their hands because they have smaller team, or it is a shorter sales process. Customers may not need as much help from salespeople, or the salespeople and customers may be in a concentrated geographical area.

Sales management compensation differs from career salesperson compensation. Sales managers, due to the length of time within the organization, will often command a higher base salary. The opportunity to have the spikes in compensation compared to that as a career salesperson is minimized, hence a reason to consider making the move to sales management. It is not the same roller coaster ride of highs and lows that is associated with the career salesperson's compensation, but more of a softer up and down roller coaster ride. Picture one that you would take small children to at the amusement park compared to the big one at the amusement park that can attract a younger demographic who enjoys the whopping, twisting roller coaster with accelerated ups and downs.

A signal that can tell you if a job is a good or great job compared to one that is not, is how long the individual stays in their current position. One of these positions is the role of Regional Sales Manager. A Regional Sales Manager is kind of in "limbo", you are away from the front line and do not have to deal with the daily customer complaints that a salesperson has to deal with; there is a level of management between you and the salesperson, and on the other side you are not in the fire the way that the Director of Sales, Vice-President of Sales, and CEO are. A Regional Sales Manager is a middle management position. For years people have been asking the question, what does middle management do, what is their role, their purpose, their function? There is nothing better than a great Regional Sales Manager job, they do not give them up and they can stay in this position for years.

As you get promoted within sales management the travel is still an issue but can change from more local and regional travel to national and global travel. As you climb the ladder and get to Director of Sales, or National Sales Manager, you are a step away from Vice-President of Sales, which is then also a step away from becoming the CEO or President of the company.

Headquarters Marketing

Sales is not for everyone, and while an entry level sales opportunity can get your foot in the door at a company, you might find that this lifestyle may not be for you. The ups and downs, the psychology of selling, the never ending quota, the travel, will take its toll and can lead to job burnout. What if you like being on this side of the company? What if there are alternative marketing tasks that excite you and can become your passion? The marketing side of a company can be a dynamic department filled with exhilarating challenges. Working in the advertising department can be a creative role in designing and delivering the message that your company wants to convey to their target audience. Sales promotion, where your directive is to create an incentive to get a customer to buy now, can be challenging. Public Relations is bursting with opportunity as companies are becoming more conscious about their corporate image.

Product management has always been a haven for career sales people to land when they decide to make the journey towards headquarters marketing. It is a safe landing place because no one has more knowledge about the company's product than a salesperson who has been selling the product in the field, who has had to deal with all related customer issues, good and bad. A product manager is a marketing job where they embrace total responsibility for a product line. A product manager is like a parent of a new born baby, where every responsibility for the care and nurturing of that baby falls at the feet of the parent. Every decision from components, or ingredients, and packaging and labeling all fall at the feet of the product manager. Products that have deep product lines, with multiple varieties and product line extensions of the original product, or product mix depth where there are complementary products can require several layers of product management including, assistant product manager, associate product manager, product manager, and senior product manager positions. Success at this role in the organization can lead to promotion to the Director of Marketing position which is a step away from becoming the Vice-President of Marketing which also is a step away from becoming the CEO or President of the company.

When you look at the above listing of career steps for the three tracks there are a few things to make note of. The career salesperson track is on the extreme left and the headquarters marketing is on the extreme right. What is meant by this is that while all of these job titles are technically on the same side of the organization there are extreme differences between the tracks. The biggest extreme to the left is freedom and independence. The career salesperson does not work a traditional nine to five schedule, typically works out of an office in their home, and is as far removed from the corporate environment as can be. Working in headquarters marketing could not be more opposite and is as far to the other extreme as you can get. Headquarters marketing is very corporate, with the traditional nine to five mentality, chained to a desk, and as ensconced in the corporate environment as can be. Sales management is in the middle, and has a taste of both worlds with their time being split between working in the field with their salespeople and working with senior management on sales related issues.

These extremes often cause friction between the sales department and the marketing department. Compensation is the first issue that causes friction. For the most part salespeople can and do make more money that marketing executives. However, the compensation for marketing executives is more consistent than that of salespeople. Salespeople are traditionally paid commission on all sales. Marketing executives are traditionally paid a salary plus a bonus on the profitability of their product. There is the rub. The salesperson just wants to make the sale, but marketing is more concerned about the profit margin on the sale. The salesperson wants to make the sale regardless of the profit margin because typically they are not paid on profitability. Another issue is the question who spends more time working? This is a hands down answer, marketing executives spend much more time at their desk and do work many more hours than salespeople. This can cause animosity especially when a salesperson calls into the office to speak with the marketing department from the golf course, or the beach, while they are stuck toiling behind a desk. Throw in the fact that the salesperson is making more money than they are, and you can see where the animosity, which borders on jealousy, can come from. Nothing burns a headquarters marketing executive more than when they hear about a huge commission check that was cut to a career salesperson for closing a big sale, or a year-end bonus check for surpassing an inflated quota that was put in place by management.

It is all about choices and options and as you can see, a career starting in sales can present many doors for you to open where you are not boxed into a career for life. Circumstances change in life, so if the travel starts to become an issue, think about moving to the marketing side. If the stress associated with selling is starting to get to you, transfer to the public relations department. If you have had enough with the specter of quota hanging over your head every day, pursue a career in advertising. The whole point is that there is flexibility, you can spend ten years in sales, ten years in sales management, and ten years in marketing. You can also spend thirty years as a career salesperson, which is your choice. You can jump back and forth, start in sales, shift to marketing, and if you find out it is not for you, shift back to sales. It is a wonderful feeling knowing that this life that you have chosen has as many career options, and has as many career paths that it does.

Section 3

Occupational Hazards

This section discusses other sales job related issues that are part of the life of a salesperson including quotas, commission plans and structures, why sales training and sales development needs to be a mentality, and the importance of ethical behavior among salespeople.

Chapter 5

Compensation: Show Me the Money

A dd compensation plans and commission structures to the list of sore spots that contribute to the head scratching and head banging when dealing with the psychology of selling. Quota has become a bad word in Corporate America. Yet the word is sprinkled all over this book. This is done on purpose, to plant the seed in the back of your mind and to constantly remind you that it never goes away. The word has a negative connotation with selling, yet this connotation was not created by salespeople, it was created and abused by sales management. In this politically correct world in which we live in, where everything has a softer tone, the word quota is being eradicated from the corporate landscape. It has been replaced with words like objective, goal, or number. The word objective does not sting as much and ring through your ears every morning when you get out of bed the way the word quota does. The word goal does not come with the stigma that the word quota does. It is similar how the job title salesman has been neutered. The word salesman carries a negative connotation as well. The word has been changed to salesperson, but on business cards it is still hard to find that title today. It has been replaced with such titles as Account Manager, Account Executive, Territory Manager, and Customer Business Representative.

The larger the company the more famous they are for the ever changing and evolving commission plan. What is a fair commission plan? All you can ask for is a fair plan. Most commission plans are not. Most are filled with unrealistic inflated quotas that on paper may look enticing but in reality they are not. Let's cut to the chase, quotas are inflated and unrealistic. This is the biggest issue that wears on you mentally. If you know that you have a chance to exceed your quota this can drive you and motivate you every day that you are out in the field selling. If you get out of bed in the morning, look yourself in the mirror, and realize that you have no chance of surpassing your quota, you are left with an empty and helpless feeling that can weigh on your psyche.

A fair quota starts with what the sales were for your territory for the previous year. Good year or bad year, you need to start with a baseline of where next year's quota should start. The next factor should be how fast, or how much, and what percentage of growth is your company experiencing. How much did the company grow last year, the past three years, five years, ten years? If your company increased sales by five percent over the previous year, then a fair quota is five percent over last year's sales, not ten percent. If your company's average growth for the past three, five, or ten years has been four percent then a four percent increase over last year's sales is fair, an eight percent increase over last year's sales is not fair. Another piece to the quota puzzle should be how is your company growing compared to the industry that you are competing in. If your industry is growing at three percent per year over last year's sales then your quota should be three percent and not six percent.

What is common and needs to be corrected by sales management is that over time salespeople will see through a hollow commission plan and realize that it is inflated so high that they will not have a chance to achieve the quota. Not making the quota will not lead to an immediate dismissal. Most companies want their salespeople to be successful because they look at you as a resource, where they have invested time and money to recruit, hire, and train you, they will at least give you a chance to make the quota. What is a successful ratio of making or not making the quota in today's inflated quota landscape? If you make the quota more than you miss the quota, you are a star and will get promoted. If you make it and miss it you can still keep your job. If you miss the quota more than you make the quota, then over time you might want to think about pursuing other opportunities.

Many companies do employ the practice where next year's quota starts where this year's sales finish. What is interesting is that once you have been established within a geographical territory you can have a read on what kind of sales year is it going to be. Often, as early as the first quarter of the year, you can have an idea if you are going to make the quota or not. That is very early in the sales year, and yes, it is possible to close sales at the end of the year to push you over the top, and yes, you can go down to the wire even on the last possible sales day of the year to limp across the finish line and make the quota; but for the most part you will know early on in the year.

If you know early in the year that you have a shot to surpass the quota you will pull out all stops to push every possible sale that you can to maximize the commission dollars in this year's compensation plan. The negative is that remember, next year's quota starts with where this year's sales finished up. If you blow the number out and have an incredible sales year, the baseline for your next year's quota will be high. This makes it difficult to have back to back successful years and a mentality of, "This year I will make it, but I know that next year I will not," can set in, and how is this beneficial to the company and the psyche of the salesperson?

The flip side is that also early in the year you can get a read that you have no chance to make the quota. That no matter how smart or hard you work, the quota is unattainable. You will find yourself working harder in the bad years. Why not palm, or sand-bag sales orders, which means hold onto sales orders or do not push them through until the new quota period starts. Tanking a sales year, meaning that if you are going to have a bad year, have a really bad year, so the next year your baseline as to where your quota starts will be more manageable. A mentality of great year, bad year sets in. Ask yourself, is it better to barely make your quota every other year and miss the quota the other years, or have three monster years and a couple of really bad years? The monster year mentality will win out and get you promoted. It is easier to remember who has hit the most home runs, and not that easy to remember who has struck out the most times. How does this benefit the salesperson or company? It does not and can be corrected by starting with a fair commission plan in the first place.

Something else to factor in or indicate if your compensation plan is fair or not is how many salespeople actually surpass the quota. If there are forty salespeople in your company, and ten or less out of the forty make the quota, then the quota was too high. A fair plan is where more than fifty to seventy-five percent of the salespeople make the quota. The more salespeople who make the quota the more fair and equitable the commission plan.

An end result of the constant territory shell game of changing geography coupled with the unrealistic and inflated quotas is that your best salespeople will become frustrated and end up leaving the company to pursue better opportunities. The best salespeople leave because they are good enough to find the better opportunity. It is similar to free agency in sports when the star player leaves because the organization is going in the wrong direction. Remember that as a sales manager, you are only as good as your salespeople. If the good to great salespeople leave what are you left with? Average and mediocre salespeople who are not good enough to move on to the better opportunity, remain. How does this benefit you as a sales manager and company when your best salespeople are walking out the door because of the aforementioned frustrations with compensation and territory alignment?

Agency Theory

Due to the pivotal importance of sales to most organizations, a high performing sales force is essential. As a result, a considerable amount of literature has been devoted to identifying the characteristics of effective compensation systems that will induce high performance. Some of this important literature has focused on control-oriented theories, including agency theory[3].

Agency theory emphasizes the importance of being able to measure performance, and addresses the distinction between measuring outcomes and behaviors. Agency theory conceptually separates behavior control and outcome control from the compensation program. Instead it makes prescriptions regarding the circumstances under which fixed (salary) and variable (commissions and other forms, such as bonuses) pay should be used to foster efficient alignment of principal and agent interests[4].

Agency theory offers significant potential for aiding in the design of compensation plans for sales personnel. Agency theory considers the desire to equate greater risk with greater reward, a concept that is predominantly germane to the utilization of incentive compensation, in the development of sales compensation programs. Agency theory argues that putting compensation at risk, as opposed to providing a salary, generally requires greater remuneration to compensate for the risk dynamic.

Agency theory is a method utilized by organizations to discover effective profit capitalization control systems. Agency theory focuses on the relationship between the principal who delegates the work, and the agent who performs the work. Components of an agency relationship include the organization, the agent (salesperson), external environmental factors, and the performance of the agent. The organization tries to influence the actions of the agent, and the organization specifically monitors these actions to insure that the agent recognizes the power that the organization has over the agent[5].

The cornerstone of this theory is the assumption that the organization and the agent have diverse objectives and agendas. The organization might want the agent, in this case a salesperson, to focus their daily selling efforts on the company's new, but unproven product. Whereas the salesperson might want to focus their daily selling efforts on existing products that have a proven track record for helping the salesperson achieve and surpass their quota.

Agency theory suggests that the problems associated with the diverse objectives and agendas of both stakeholders must be brought in alignment with each other. It is the responsibility of the organization to create compensation plans that align the objectives and agendas of the agent, (salesperson) with the interests of the organization. Agency theory addresses ways in which compensation can be used to align their divergent interests and goals[6].

Agency theory has been found to be a useful predictor of the types of sales compensation systems. A study of salespeople concluded that salespeople with highly programmed sales jobs can be trained very quickly, they could be monitored easily, and tended toward salary compensation. Salespeople with low programmability sales jobs can also be paid a salary, but used a high level of continuing supervision to maintain control. In alignment with agency theory concepts, salespeople with low programmability jobs needed less supervision but emphasized commissions[7].

Additional researchers applied agency theory in the area of sales force compensation[8]. Agency theory suggests that basing compensation on any form of commission based program may not be a recommended practice unless it is probable to establish logically accurate outcome measures that cover every expectation established by sales management. The researchers modeled the optimal structure of a compensation plan in terms of its fixed (behavior control) and variable (outcome control) components. The proposed model suggests the weaker the link between salespeople's effort and sales results, the higher the proportion of compensation that should be fixed (i.e., salary-based). Agency theory suggests that if desired behaviors are identified and monitored at minimal cost, sales management should base compensation primarily on salary. When these conditions are not met, then sales management should design compensation programs that are in alignment with desired outcomes.

In this case, salespeople are at high risk because their efforts do not result predictably to the desired outcomes. Hence, it is less costly to the firm to assume the risk (via salary) than to pay high commission rates to compensate the salespeople for the risk assumed. The ratio of salary compensation to commission compensation will increase with increases in the level of environmental uncertainty.

Compensation experts stress the need to continually adjust any variable-pay structure to reflect the current business environment[9]. The compensation plan that was implemented only a couple of years ago, may today reward activity that is no longer important to the company's current business direction. This is a myth, when in fact marketing executives wrestle with this annual problem and are searching for models of compensation plans that they can implement into their own organizations.

Contemporary sales strategy focuses on relationship selling as opposed to traditional methods, which focused on the transaction itself. In other words, transaction selling focuses on making the sale today, and worry about your relationship with your customer tomorrow. Today the transaction approach does not fold into the landscape of selling in the marketplace of the new millennium. If relationship selling focuses on the long-term relationship between customer and company, how can you consistently change the rules with regards to incentive compensation?

If companies are preaching relationship selling, then compensation programs should not be altered, changed, or modified as readily as described in the above example. Developing relationships with customers cannot be done overnight. It takes an implausible amount of time to develop relationships with customers. Just as the salesperson establishes a relationship with a customer, the company pulls the rug out on the salesperson, and decides to shift the direction and emphasis of the compensation plan.

Turnover, or the rate that employees leave an organization, is a fantastic way to gauge what kind of company you work for. Even during the interview process it is a great question to ask a sales manager, "How long have you been with the company? How long have the other members of your sales team or sales region been with the company?" If the majority of the salespeople in your region have been there a relatively short time (less than three years), this might be a signal that the quota is too high and unachievable, and either the salesperson leaves or is dismissed because they cannot surpass the quota. Hence, if the answer is that the majority of the salespeople have been with the company for many years (more than five years), can be a sign that the quota is realistic. It is also imperative to ask have many times they have made their quota. If the answer is frequently then this is a message that the good to great salespeople are staying with the organization. If the answer is that there is inconsistent sale performance by your teammates, then this is a signal that they are not good enough to find a more attractive opportunity. It is an outstanding way to measure how your sales manager will manage your performance. A micro-manager will churn and burn, and turnover their sales roster too frequently. The manager that you want to work for will have loyal sales representatives who enjoy working for their sales manager.

Additional issues that will arise and can affect your performance versus your quota is the availability of products, the time it takes to bring new products to market, and problems with the performance or quality of current products. When does a sale become a sale? When you convince the customer to say yes, shake your hand and issue you a purchase order? Is it when your company receives the purchase order, is it when the company ships the product? Is it when the product is received or when the customer pays the bill? For the record, the hardest part of all of the above mentioned activities is the first one, convincing the customer to say yes, "I will take it." That is when the sale should be recorded and the commission should be paid at that moment. Your job is to obtain the purchase order and you should be paid upon receipt of the purchase order. Good luck with that. The worst situation is to be paid your commission when your customer pays the bill. If the customer takes ninety days to pay the bill you have to wait three months for your commission. What if they never pay the bill, you will not receive a dollar in commission for all of the hard work that you had to endure to convince your customer to say, "I'll take it." The customary way to record a sale is the date when a product gets shipped off of the loading dock from your company and is on its way to the customer. If nothing gets shipped today, nothing gets recorded as a sale.

Back orders are another sore spot for salespeople. A back order exists when you make a sale but your company is out of stock of the item, so the sale does not get credited to you and you will not receive your commission until the product is in stock. How much does this hurt? What if you are in the last week of the quota period and you are below your quota and only have a few days left to achieve and surpass the quota. If you make the sale you will not only receive the commission on the sale but a bonus for surpassing the quota. You convince a customer to place an order today and obtain all of the necessary paperwork to push the sale through including a signed purchase order. Only to find out that your company is out of stock on the product and the order does not get shipped. The customer never receives the delivery, you lose credibility with your customer because you guaranteed the delivery if they place the order that day. The customer buys the product from your competitor who ships it out immediately. You lose the sale, do not make your quota for the period, miss out on the bonus, and have to explain to your sales manager why you did not make the quota. Ouch! The corporate response that you will often hear is that at least you will start the next quota period off on a good foot, or that you should not have waited until the end of the quota period to push through sales at the wire, or absolute end of the quota period.

New product development is essential to stay competitive in today's marketplace. The time it takes to convert an idea for a new product to something that can be sold, or the time it takes to bring a product to market can be longer than expected. However, this anticipated new product is often included in your quota for the upcoming period. What if the product is not available, delayed by research and development, the Food and Drug Administration (FDA) or some other government regulation that can slow down the release of your product? What if your product has manufacturing defects and is recalled? Quota never gets adjusted for these delays, you are still responsible to deliver a number. You are not part of the research and development team who made the mistakes that are causing the delays, yet you are held to a quota that escapes other departments in the organization. What happens if your current model is out of date and your customers are having problems with defective products and your solution is to purchase your new model which has addressed and corrected all of these manufacturing issues? What if production becomes delayed because a glitch or bug in the manufacturing process is discovered further delaying release of the product? Not only will you have an unhappy customer on your hands who will begin to entertain the offers from your competitors, but you will also have your sales manager breathing down your neck asking you why are you not making your quota.

You, as the salesperson, are the representative for the company and who the customer visualizes. As they say in sports you are the face of the franchise. The corporate people get to hide in the headquarters. Customers do not see the face of the manufacturing manager, or research and development engineer, or even CEO who made the decision to cut back on production in lieu of a more favorable stock price, they see you, and you have to face the music. People buy from people they like and the last thing that you want is to compromise your integrity as a salesperson, because once you compromise your integrity with a customer you will never get it back.

Forms of Compensation

Benefit packages and expenses are both forms of compensation, and this can vary from company to company. There is a significant price tag associated with benefit packages, and how expenses are reimbursed can separate one job opportunity from another. This section is designed to focus on the monetary side of compensation. Compensation is such a sore spot because it always comes down to the money. The sore spot is not necessarily the amount of money but the terms of the compensation plan and the constant changing of the compensation plan. What is the optimal form of compensation, what is optimal for the company and what is optimal for the salesperson?

Straight Salary

Straight salary means exactly what it says, the salesperson is paid a fixed amount of money and is compensated like any traditional non-sales related employee. It is straightforward to administer, and simple to budget for because it is a fixed expense. The salesperson is paid their salary regardless of how much revenue they generate. The advantage to the salesperson is the security associated with the guarantee that they will receive a paycheck during whatever pay period the company works under, weekly, bi-monthly, or monthly. Motivating the salesperson can be a challenge because they are compensated regardless if the sale is consummated or not. Straight salary does reduce the incidence of unethical behavior because the salesperson is not inclined to stretch the truth, because they are not receiving commission on the sale. A way to motivate the salesperson under this form of compensation is that if the salesperson surpasses their assigned quota they receive a substantial raise in their base salary the following year. Tying in salary increases to quota performance is an excellent way to keep the salesperson motivated. Put in place a sliding scale that the greater the quota achievement, the higher the salary increase, with the caveat that a subpar quota achievement warrants a subpar salary increase.

An advantage to the salesperson of this form of compensation is if you are a new salesperson, not necessarily new to personal selling but new to a product, industry, or market. This form of compensation can help build confidence in a salesperson and allow them to nurture and develop their selling skills. A company can have a longer leash when it comes to salesperson performance because a company has invested resources in the salesperson and is more apt to give the salesperson a chance to be successful. Sales management control and accountability is at the highest under straight salary compensation programs. Since a salary is paid regardless of a sale being made, can open the door for the micro-management of the salesperson. An advantage of the straight salary compensation plan can be if additional non-selling time is needed which can include a lengthened sales cycle, training of customers, installation and implementation of the product, or other service and follow-up activities this will irritate a salesperson who can view these activities as a loss of valuable selling time. The straight salary salesperson does not see this as a loss of valuable selling time that can impact their ability to earn more commission but as an opportunity to learn their craft and enhance the development of the relationship with their customer. The disadvantage of this form of compensation is what if you are a great salesperson? The great salesperson is hampered by this form of compensation because they are not maximizing their ability, and the sales volume that they are generating exceeds the straight salary that they are receiving.

Straight Commission

Straight commission is precisely what it is defined as. A salesperson is compensated only by commission. No sale means no commission.

No sale means no money. This is at the other end of the spectrum compared to the straight salary compensation plan. The advantage to the company is that there is less of an investment in the salesperson, salespeople are paid a percentage of what they sell, so compensation is only earned when a sale is completed. Salesperson compensation is not necessarily budgeted as a fixed expense, but more of a variable expense that goes up when sales go up and down when sales go down. A negative is that a company might not be as tolerant with regards to sales performance because there is minimal investment and the long-term commitment to the development of the salesperson is not present.

What is the advantage for a salesperson to work under a straight commission compensation plan? What if you are a seasoned sales professional with a network of clients and a proven sales history of successful selling? Straight commission compensation plans offer the highest possible percentage of commission possible. If you are a great salesperson, and you are extremely confident in your ability as a salesperson, the straight commission plan can be maximized under this form of compensation. The downside are business and economic downturns that are out of control of the salesperson can create more of a roller coaster ride when it comes to compensation. Freedom and independence is optimized under a straight commission compensation program, there is less hand holding and less of a chance for micro-managing to creep in. Sales management has less control over not only the activity of a straight commissioned salesperson but the direction and focus of their sales activity.

Straight salary salespeople have no choice but to follow the direction of sales management specifically when it comes to what products to sell and which type of customer to call on. Straight commission salespeople make sales calls on customers who they have the best chance of selling a product to and push products that they know they can sell. This is different from following corporate directives which dictate how a salesperson should spend their time, specifically when a new and unproven product is launched into the marketplace. A destructive consequence of straight commission is that the opportunity for unethical behavior is heightened. A straight commission salesperson is more tempted to stretch the truth in order to make the sale. Sales management supervision and accountability is diminished furthering the chance of unethical claims that a salesperson can make during their presentation in front of a customer. A massive issue that must be raised under this form of compensation is how frequent are sales being made. The salesperson selling a disposable product where consistent repeat sales are made is the optimal situation for a straight commission plan. Sales are more routine and more frequent therefore compensation can be more predictable. The opposite is the case as well. If sales are not as frequent, and possibly larger but spread out over time where the sales cycle is not as routine and extended, can contribute to the peak and valley lifestyle associated with a straight commission compensation program.

A method of alleviating the pain associated with the straight commission program is for a company to offer a "draw versus commission" plan. A draw versus commission means that a salesperson receives compensation before a sale is made. Their compensation is a stipend against anticipated commissions that are earned in the future. This is common for new salespeople starting at a company to give them an opportunity to build up a client base and develop relationships with customers until a steady flow of sales are generated. Most draw versus commission plans are short-term, usually less than one year, and the draw can be reduced on a monthly basis until it disappears and then the salesperson is on a straight commission program.

Salary Plus Commission and Bonus

While there are certainly advantages and disadvantages of both the straight salary and straight commission compensation programs the extreme end of either program can be problematic. The straight commission salesperson has an entrepreneurship mentality while the straight salary salesperson thinks more as a company employee. A solution is to slide the scale of compensation towards the middle and utilize the advantages of both compensation plans and minimize the negatives associated with each form of compensation. Many companies have instituted some form of a combination compensation plan that provides a base salary, plus commission, and bonuses. This can be the best of both worlds. This type of compensation brings all extremes towards the middle. Salespeople are given a base salary but have the incentive and motivation to earn more compensation by selling more products. It evens out the peaks and valleys by providing a salary and allows for a more consistent flow of compensation.

A question that needs to be clarified is when does the commission function of the combination plan kick in? The most advantageous combination programs pay commission starting at "dollar one." This is imperative to find out as a salesperson. Dollar one means that the salesperson receives commission on every dollar that they sell. Some combination programs do not start to pay commission until a threshold of sales has been achieved. That is not optimal for the salesperson, because in essence you are a straight salary employee until a certain level of sales achievement is reached. Some combination compensation programs start commission at a low percentage and escalate as sales increase. The fair plan to have is one that pays the same percentage of commission from dollar one and then escalates once the quota is achieved. This gives incentive for the salesperson to surpass the quota. This is a fair plan for the company as well, because the higher commission is only paid after the salesperson exceeds the often unrealistic quota that has been put in place.

A goal of the combination plan is to spread out compensation. A base salary does that, but when commission is actually paid is more complicated. From a company's perspective think of commission as a pie. When do you dish out a piece of the pie? Do you dish out minimal pieces more frequently or do you dish out more substantial pieces less frequently. Salespeople want their commission earned on a sale, yesterday. Every good salesperson starts calculating their commission the minute a sale is closed. That is a healthy mentality. A concern is when is commission actually paid? Some companies do not believe in the same philosophy of paying commission the minute after the sale is closed, some in fact can take MONTHS, not minutes to reward their salespeople. The corporate stance is that if commission was paid to every salesperson the day that the sale was completed it would cause an accounting nightmare for the company. Just as technology has helped salespeople in the field, the same applies for accounting personnel as well, there are accounting software programs designed to speed up the process of when commission is paid to salespeople. A key question that must be understood is when does a company recognize when commission is paid. The optimal situation is to pay commission based on when a product is shipped. Some companies pay commission AFTER the customer pays for the product. This is the worst situation to be in because commission will not be paid until the bill is paid which can take months.

It goes back to what is a fair plan. A fair plan pays out commission to salespeople the following month after all sales minus customer returns are calculated. The commission that a salesperson earns this month should be the net sales for the salesperson's territory from the following month. Some companies pay out commission every quarter, so salespeople really only receive a commission check four times a year. Some companies hold a percentage of a salesperson's commission for an annual end of the year payout. This does not spread out compensation. Why does a company withhold commissions for an extended time period way after the sale was made? For one reason and one reason only. It forces the salesperson to remain with the company until they receive their full commission. If a salesperson leaves a company before the end of a quota period the company is not obligated to pay out the balance of the commission. This is often outlined in the hard copy of the compensation plan that the company distributes at the beginning of the year, which often places a date that a salesperson has to be gainfully employed by the company to receive their commission. A salesperson has to sign and agree to the terms of the compensation program otherwise their employment can be in jeopardy.

Another way to spread out compensation is to offer additional bonuses that go beyond commission payments that are based on a percentage of sales. Competition among salespeople can create a healthy competitive atmosphere that can motivate salespeople. Most companies distribute actual rankings of salespeople, or if you will, sales standings, very similar to how teams are ranked in sports. This does create a first place, last place mentality. This is healthy because it acknowledges and rewards the top achievers and motivates the underachievers to elevate their place in the sales standings. It is common for a company to form a President's Club that honors and recognizes the top quota achievers for a given year. Cash rewards can be given to members of the club. Companies offer exotic and lavish trips (compensation) to President Club winners. Not all of the salespeople in the company are invited on the trip, just the President's Club winners. It can become a notch on the belt mentality, "How many times have you been a President's Club winner?" This is an excellent motivational tool that can act as an incentive (compensation) to surpass your quota and get recognized among your peers.

Sales contests for monthly or quarterly quota achievement, sales contests that are product specific that reward performance for selling the most of a specific product, or for sales of a new product are all common. Another word for this practice is a "spiff", a spiff is a short term form of compensation that can spur sales for a specific product. Spiff's often occur when sales are sluggish and an infusion or focus on a specific product is needed to help jump start sales. Remember a company does budget and have a pie set aside for sales compensation for the year, and money is often left in the budget. A way to utilize the allotted budgeted dollars is to create some form of incentive compensation program that salespeople can take advantage of and supplement their compensation.

Successful companies who have a proven method of success often attempt to mold their employees and guide them in the direction towards what has worked in the past for other prosperous employees. This can be a recipe for success for salespeople as well. Management by Objectives (MBO) is a management philosophy that can enhance the performance of salespeople and also become a form of compensation. Once the blueprint of success is established it can be disseminated to the salespeople in the field. If this formula includes making a certain amount of sales calls each day, every day, the chance of making a sale can be increased. An MBO program means following the established blueprint, and if the salesperson follows that blueprint they can receive a bonus for their activity in the field. It gets the salesperson in the mode of making a certain amount of sales calls every day. It encourages a robotic, cookie-cutter approach towards selling. The residual effect of the MBO is to create a mindset of what is needed to be done to be successful as a salesperson. It develops a work ethic and a routine that if followed properly can lead to an increase in the performance of the salesperson.

A solution to the compensation dilemma, which includes the animosity built up between salespeople and their company with regards to the shell game of compensation and unfair and inflated quotas, is to give the salesperson the option to select the compensation program that best meets their needs. Some salespeople can benefit from the straight salary program, while others can benefit from the straight commission plan, yet others may be more comfortable with the combination compensation plan. This takes the onus off the company and puts the onus on the salesperson, they are given the option to choose the compensation plan that suits their needs. This reduces the aforementioned compensation animosity. There are some conditions that are only fair. A time frame for the chosen plan has to be established. It cannot be a brief time frame either. It cannot allow for a salesperson to maximize the compensation plan under straight commission for one year and then switch to straight salary the following year because their quota will be unattainable following the successful year. The reverse guideline should also be in place where a salesperson cannot work on straight salary for one year then switch to straight commission because they can anticipate a monster sales year is on the horizon.

Chapter 6

Sales Training and Sales Development: Even Superman had Kryptonite

Salespeople engage in relationships with customers that require the transfer of knowledge. This knowledge base includes product, company, competitive, market, and industry knowledge, that is transferred to the customer during the sales process. How do salespeople acquire this knowledge? What are the effective practices that sales management can utilize in maximizing their training resources? The goals of sales training initiatives are to develop productive salespeople. Sales management is challenged with selecting a sales training methodology that can bear effective results. Sales training and sales development is a corporate mentality or belief. Some companies view their salespeople as a resource that needs to be nurtured and cultivated, others are not as committed to the cause. Sales training and sales development, while related, are not the same exercise. Sales training is for today, the present, and sales development is for tomorrow or the future. Sales training is more of an initial orientation that can include product training, but can be extended to include training on company policies, company history, competitive products, and the improvement of basic selling skills. Sales development is more of an enhancement of the initial orientation and can include a deeper dive into advanced selling techniques, customer relationship skills, new technology that can make you more efficient as a salesperson, or more professional ways of carrying yourself as a salesperson.

One of the few characteristics of business, that is an absolute assurance, is that the business marketplace is an ever changing dynamic. Dramatic changes are occurring in management theory, and equal shifts need to occur as well in sales training and sales development. Traditionally the perspective of sales training has been focused on outcomes related to a particular job task. Sales development has been centered on individual growth and enrichment.

The direction of sales training has undergone dramatic shifts from product specific training, to customer needs driven training. This shift has led to the increase in ethics training, customer needs assessment, and more of a problem solving approach to selling. The role of the salesperson is to become more of a source of information to customers. The role of an intelligence gatherer for the buyer requires gathering information pertaining to the buyer's needs. In order for the salesperson to perform roles as intelligence gatherers on behalf of customers, sales training programs need to emphasize certain skills. Salespeople should be taught how and where to look for possible sources of information in the buyer's markets[10].

Research suggests that the dynamic nature of the industrial market environment is such that industrial marketers will have to constantly monitor shifts in the marketplace to identify emerging trends that may significantly alter existing sales force roles. The ability to accurately forecast changes in customer expectations will enhance the ability of the seller to devise effective strategies to cope with these changes[11].

Sales training and sales development need to be taken to new heights. The bar and expectations for sales training and sales development must be raised. Recommendations include the development of a new framework for sales training and sales development that focuses on the concept of the knowledge economy. Companies which embrace knowledge management into their corporate cultures will remain consistent with similar paradigm shifts occurring in today's marketplace.

Sales training and sales development is an investment by your company in your success as a salesperson. It can be a signal when you have to make a decision as to which company to accept a job offer with. One company can have an extensive and on-going sales training and sales development program and another company can believe, or have a mentality, that it is someone else's responsibility to train and develop you. Some companies do not want to make the investment and choose to hire experienced salespeople, while yes, they hire salespeople who have already proven themselves as a salesperson, they also can arrive at a company with some baggage, or selling techniques that need to be revisited. The company with the mentality that training is an investment in their salespeople might be the more advantageous place to be, that they value their salespeople as a human resource and have an interest in your long-term success. Sales management wants you to be successful as a salesperson, if you are successful, they are successful, and they want to give their salespeople the best opportunity to succeed and it all starts with a solid foundation that begins with sales training.

Sales training and sales development does not come cheap, and salespeople need to take advantage of the opportunity. Either way salespeople should embrace sales training and sales development because it can improve your performance as a salesperson. Improved performance can lead to improved sales, which means more commission for the salesperson, so why would a salesperson bristle at the opportunity to become a more well rounded professional salesperson? The resistance comes from seasoned salespeople who have the attitude that they have been there and done that, and they are old dogs who cannot be trained to perform new tricks. This is a mistake, sales development is an ongoing process, the day that a salesperson believes that they cannot learn any new selling techniques is the day that their sales career can slowly begin to head downhill. A mentality that salespeople are lifelong learners needs to be ingrained into all salespeople. Business changes every day and the selling techniques that were practiced in the past, while possibly successful, might not work in today's dynamic selling environment.

When Should Formal Sales Training Take Place?

When is the best time to deliver sales training? The first day on the job? Or after a salesperson has spent some time in the field with customers? It is an interesting debate with advantages and disadvantages of both approaches. The advantage of initiating sales training on the first day of employment is that the slate is clean, the salesperson has no preconceived notions about the job, and they can be molded into a company way of thinking. The disadvantage is that the salesperson has not been exposed to the field and it can be difficult to apply concepts that are emphasized during the training. Initial product training can be intensive, overwhelming, and confusing. If your first day on the job is in a training class it is common for a new salesperson to be confused and lost because an overload of product information is being crammed into your head rather quickly.

The advantage of starting your first day in the field is that you are live in front of the customer and can benefit from an "on the job" experience. The salesperson can see firsthand the features and the benefits of the product, and obtain immediate customer feedback. Once the formal sales training commences the salesperson can relate the initial field sales experience with the content that is delivered during the formal sales training. The sales training content can be easily digested and be more effective because the salesperson can apply what was experienced in the field and what was taught during the sales training process.

What usually determines when you will be trained has as much to do with when you are hired as with anything else. Companies need to fill a training class and if you are the first salesperson hired in the training class you might be spending some time in the field before your class convenes. If you are the last salesperson in the training class hired you may spend zero days in the field and your first day on the job you can find yourself in a training class. If turnover of salespeople is low it can take months to be formally trained. If turnover is high, or if the company is going through an expansion where a block of new salespeople are being hired relatively at the same time, the training process can be accelerated.

Measuring the Effectiveness of Sales Training

Within the landscape of Corporate America, there has been a movement towards viewing sales training as a necessary ingredient in the long-term success of the organization. Having more of a customer focus, where customer satisfaction and customer service are paramount to the organization, is becoming more of the rule than exception in Corporate America. This shift has prompted more of an emphasis on the effectiveness of sales training. Salespeople are on the front line, with direct access and visibility to customers. It is obvious that there is a need to have salespeople, with this direct contact to customers, to be properly trained and equipped to solve customer related issues in the field.

This focus has led to increases in corporate funding for sales training[12]. Companies are placing more of an emphasis on the effectiveness of sales training. As the price of sales training per employee continues to soar, it is becoming more evident that measuring the effectiveness of sales training is becoming a challenge to determine. This increase in funding has led to the necessary analysis of the sales training initiative. In order to measure the effectiveness of sales training, you must be able to measure a sales trainee's level of satisfaction with the sales training that they have received.

Researchers have argued that the real world constraints and pressures of business hinder the development of a textbook approach to planning sales training. Research findings state that a primary source of input used in the identification of training needs is sales management[13]. A request by sales management for a particular sales training program may signal an urgency to resolve certain sales force performance problems. Given this perceived urgency, the sales training department might forego additional formalized input regarding the nature and type of sales training needed in an attempt to quickly respond to senior management[14].

Research suggests that there is not enough focus on the needs of the sales trainee, the focus is on the process of sales training in general. This can create a void in the learning process, the content of the sales training that is being delivered, is not what is actually needed by the sales trainee. The sales trainee is therefore not learning what is necessary to become successful.

In order to effectively assess the needs of the sales trainee, sales training should focus on three primary areas: the organization, the task, and the individual[15]. From a sales training perspective, sales trainee needs, with regard to the task that is to be performed needs to be the focal point of the sales training. Task assessment analyzes the sales job and includes three phases: specifying behavioral activities and duties required, identifying and prioritizing actual steps involved in accomplishing duties, and the determination of topical areas to be covered in sales training to ensure that requisite knowledge, skills, and abilities are developed[16].

It is recommended that sales management should set the parameters of the sales training program, and the corporate sales trainers should determine the content. The content delivered must be in response to the needs of the salesperson in the field. This should not be an assumption of the sales training department, but a reaction from feedback and evaluations of salespeople in the field. If you are assessing needs, go to the source, in this case salespeople in the field.

From a sales training perspective a factor that has been identified that can measure the effectiveness of sales training is that the more prior experience the sales trainee has, the more effective the training program. Sales trainees having previous sales experience will be better able to relate to the sales training material than those with minimal sales experience. Their familiarity with field sales will facilitate their understanding of the sales training information and allow them to use it more quickly and adeptly than sales trainees with little or no sales experience[17]. This corresponds with research that found that adult learners, because of their broad range of experiences, will assign relatively strong meaning to new ideas and skills and that the more explicit the associations are between the old and new knowledge, the deeper and more permanent the learning (training) will be[18].

However, sales experience can hinder a salesperson's ability to learn new skills. Accepted sales management practice includes giving an individual an opportunity to develop their own style and delivery of selling skills. Based on the nature of the job description of field selling, and due to the fact that a significant amount of time is spent alone in the field, it makes sense to allow a salesperson to develop their own style of selling. The end result of this freedom enables the salesperson to develop a comfort level as to what works for them in a given selling environment. Salespeople will tend to gravitate towards previous success. When the experienced salesperson is forced into a new learning environment, whether it is to sell a new product, or when an experienced salesperson enters a new and different industry, the previous habits can act as a reference point. The previous selling habit can prejudice what is trying to be learned.

A function of sales training is to replicate the selling environment. Sales training reinforces successful selling practices. There must be a connection between the content of the sales training being delivered, with what the salesperson is experiencing in the field. If the sales training that is being delivered does not answer questions that are being raised in the field, the salesperson does not make the connection.

In order to experience satisfaction you need to perceive value. Value in the context of sales training relates to how does the sales training help me solve problems that I am experiencing in the field. If the sales training does not answer these questions, the salesperson does not perceive value in the sales training. Low perception of value leads to low levels of satisfaction.

Sales management must not ignore the salesperson's feedback and evaluation of sales training. Sales management needs to listen more to the needs of salespeople. If the sales training responds to the needs of the salesperson, and the salesperson is now able to solve previous problems, the salesperson will experience the value of the sales training and have a higher level of satisfaction.

Due to the increased importance of sales training to an organization, and the increases in resources allocated for sales training, it has become apparent that an evaluation mechanism must be implemented to ensure proper return on investment.

From a sales training perspective an audit of the sales training program can help identify and correct actual and potential sales training shortcomings. In other words, gaps in the learning process can be identified, and refocused on for future sales training exercises. The audit allows sales management to take a step back, and view the effectiveness and efficiency of the sales training through a different lens. An analysis of the company's internal and external environment, needs assessment of the sales trainee, objectives of the sales training, and evaluation and follow-up are all necessary components that must be addressed by the audit.

A sales training audit dissects the entire sales training process. This dissection places learning under a microscope. Is the content of the material being delivered a match for what is needed to be successful, once the sales trainee exits the sales training program and goes into the field. If the audit reveals that there is a disconnect between what is being taught, and what is needed to be successful, the content of what is being delivered must be adjusted to meet the needs of the salesperson in the field.

Sales Training Formats

Sales training and sales development can be delivered in many formats. The more utilization of the available formats, the more of a commitment to sales training and sales development by your company. The more formats of sales training and sales development that are utilized the higher the price tag is for sales training and sales development. Sales training formats include classroom training, on-line training, vestibule training, and field sales training.

Classroom training is a traditional format where a group of salespeople are assembled in a conference room or corporate training center. The advantage of this format is that the sales trainer has the most control. The sales trainer can control the content of the training, and can control the flow and schedule of the training. A large volume of training content can be delivered in this format. The downside is that the training is not live, the training is manufactured, and can lack the real world feeling. Classroom training can be costly, if you have a training class with new salespeople from all corners of the country, logistically having them fly into a central location for the training, the cost of hotels, meals, and entertainment can escalate quickly. Another issue that seems to be overlooked is that classroom training follows a typical nine to five schedule. Salespeople are out in the field every day and loathe the concept of the nine to five mentality. During this format the salespeople are sitting for most of the day. Salespeople are not used to sitting around all day, they are on their feet, on the move, in the car, out of the car, and are not programmed for the nine to five, sit at a desk lifestyle. The result is that the sales trainer can lose the attention of the audience, especially with a schedule that is jammed with massive amounts of content that can confuse the salesperson.

The advent of technology has taken the traditional format of classroom training and has morphed the content into on-line training. Most companies today have integrated some form of web based training into their sales training programs. While there is an upfront cost associated with creating the content it can be cost effective. Salespeople can access the training from their home office and dramatically reduces the cost associated with travel, meals, and entertainment. If some of the classroom training has to be delivered face-to-face, but some does not, companies are front loading the training with the on-line training first, then followed up by the formal traditional classroom environment. An example would be that previously the classroom training was a two week exercise. Today that can be cut in half, one week virtual and one week traditional classroom, that reduces the expense significantly. Videoconferencing can be utilized where the sales trainer is still in the classroom but the salespeople are connected virtually. What is appealing about this format is that the training can be delivered in modules, where the salesperson can go back and listen to a segment that they are not sure about. A disadvantage of the on-line format is that the sales trainer does not know the level of attention that the salesperson is giving during the training. In a classroom environment if a salesperson is not paying attention, or dozing off during a presentation, the sales trainer will know immediately. A method to insure attentiveness during the on-line format is to interject the training with pop quizzes that ask questions about content that was recently covered.

A shortcoming of classroom and on-line training is that it is still not an exact portrayal of what the job is like in the field. "On-the-job" training, where the sales trainee is thrown out in the field and asked to figure it out, can be effective, but does come with significant risks. The sales trainee is not qualified to answer questions and can make mistakes that can be costly. What if a salesperson misinforms a customer about the use of a product and an accident occurs? In the case of the medical device industry, what if a surgeon asks a new salesperson if a product can used for this type of surgical procedure, but it really does not have that application? You can see this can be a recipe for disaster. How can this be avoided? Vestibule training is the answer. Vestibule training includes the simulation or recreation of a live event. This is an effective method of training but extremely expensive. The goal of vestibule training is to get as close to the live event as possible. The closer to the live event the better. The closer to recreation of the event, the more expensive the training. How are people trained to fly planes, drive tractor trailers, navigate ships into a port? It is done on a simulator. High-tech vestibule training can give the trainee the experience necessary to avoid mistakes and is an effective method of training.

Field sales training, where the new salesperson spends time in the field with an experienced, successful salesperson from another territory is an excellent and effective method of sales training. The goal is to tie in content from the classroom, and on-line sessions, with the real world experience of being in the field. This method is extremely effective for one reason, it is live, it is real. The directive of a field sales trainer is to have the sales trainee experience what a typical day or week is like in the field. Usually this can be accomplished in a two week time frame. Two full weeks in the field is optimal, usually most customer interactions good and bad will come up during the two weeks. The sales trainee needs to see exactly what their job will be like and what they can expect during the field training assignment. The cost associated with this is relatively low, only the travel expense of the sales trainee, and typically the sales trainer will receive a stipend for their facilitation of the training assignment.

A drawback to this format is that while the products are the same that the field sales trainer and sales trainee are selling, to the same type of customer, the market can differ. If you have a sales trainer from a North Eastern market training a sales trainee from the South West results of the field sales training can be skewed. Customers in the North East are not the same as customers in the South West and vice versa, they have different product needs. Why would sales management do this? There is a belief in sales training to send a new sales trainee into a difficult market, where maybe it is extremely competitive, or the customers are exceedingly difficult, this way they see the worst side and most challenging side of what their job is actually like on a daily basis. When they return to their own territory they can have an easier transition into the field. The opposite scenario is true as well. If you send a sales trainee into a market where it is not as competitive, and the customers are more friendly and receptive to the field sales trainer or the company, it can give a false sense of security. When the sales trainee returns to their market the reception that they receive from their customers might not be as cozy or warm. The optimal situation is to find a field sales trainer in the same market as the sales trainee. The customers will have similar needs and everyone speaks the same language.

Mentor/Mentee Relationships

Another goal of field sales training is for the sales trainee and field sales trainer to form some sort of bond and mentor/mentee relationship. Many times new salespeople need an outlet, a confidant, and many times it is not beneficial for this individual to be their sales manager. New salespeople need somewhere to go with questions or concerns. Who better to field these questions or concerns but someone who has the same exact job that they have? The experienced field sales trainer can feel the pain that the sales trainee is going through because they have been there. Mentoring is a developmental mechanism. A developmental mechanism provides assistance for the enhancement of the worker's career development and experiences within the workplace.

Selling is a challenging career. Successful selling is an ever-changing dynamic. Corporate sales training curricula offer possible solutions to daily sales and customer related problems. Sales training curricula offer the textbook solution for solving the problem. This solution often does not resolve the issue that you are encountering in the field.

Peer mentoring can act as the mechanism to resolve the issue, and solve the problem. Peer mentoring transpires when a more established salesperson (Field Sales Trainer), assumes the responsibility of enhancement and guidance of the less established salesperson.

This is a different relationship from traditional organizational hierarchies. A peer mentoring relationship can provide the solution for the problem by providing a perspective from the field. What is unique about peer mentoring is that the mentor and mentee walk in the same shoes. Current problems that the mentor faces in the field are similar to the problems that the mentee is facing. Therefore, there is a connection in the relationship. A corporate sales trainer, or sales manager might be able to understand what the mentee is experiencing, but they are, for the most part, removed from the daily field selling activities. They might have been in the field five years ago, before they were promoted to trainer or sales manager. Trainers and sales managers revert to when they were in the field. This allows for a disconnect in the relationship. The message received from the peer mentor can provide the connection and solution that the mentee is looking for. Peer mentoring can articulate formal classroom training with practical implications. From a sales training perspective, peer mentoring can act as an effective mechanism in the increase in cognition, or learning, of the mentee.

Sales Training for Sales Managers

A natural progression along the career path of a salesperson is the option to eventually move into sales management. It is a logical progression, but the daily activities of a salesperson are a stark comparison to the daily activities of a sales manager. A salesperson's daily focus is on selling products, satisfying customers, and attempting to surpass their sales quota. A sales manager's daily focus is on managing a salesperson's activity, disseminating information handed down by upper sales management, along with other managerial activities associated with the job description.

Salespeople often have difficulty making a successful transition from salesperson to sales manager[19]. When corporations think of sales training, they think of training salespeople to sell products. Often neglected is the training of the newly appointed and promoted ex-salesperson, who now holds the title of sales manager.

Research attempted to establish the existing condition of sales management training from the perspective of sales managers. The purpose of the research was to empirically examine the climate of sales management training as perceived by sales managers who have received the training.

A sample of six hundred sales managers from corporations of varied size and diverse industries were asked to respond to questions in the following areas:

1) Availability and timing of sales management training
2) Characteristics of the sales management training
3) Sales managers' perspectives of the topics covered in the training
4) Skills or abilities considered most important for success in sales management
5) Sales managers' evaluations of their own training

Fifty-seven percent of the respondents reported that their company failed to provide them with formal sales management training after their promotion to sales manager. Forty-two percent of the respondents who did receive sales management training, reported that they received the training only after they had risen to senior sales management positions, such as Regional Sales Manager, Director of Sales, and Vice-President of Sales. The research also revealed that most training that is offered for sales managers is in the form of "on-the-job" coaching by superiors or peers. This is more of an informal training, as opposed to the training of salespeople which is more structured and formalized.

Conclusions of this research confirm that training for sales managers remains an area of neglect. This empirical investigation wanted to determine the current status of sales training, from the perspective of sales managers. The results are not encouraging. The researchers suggest that reasons for this neglect are the fact that most times when a salesperson makes the progression into sales management, they have been successful as a salesperson, and making the transition into management should be a seamless transition[20]. It is not a seamless transition because the daily focus as a salesperson is "selling", whereas the daily function of sales management is not "selling" but "managing." Until management recognizes this paradigm shift in responsibility, the gap in training for sales managers will continue to exist.

Future Direction of Sales Training and Sales Development

A purpose of sales training is to increase the knowledge of salespeople in order to be more productive in the field. With more of a commitment by sales management in the area of sales training, and sales development, a need has surfaced regarding the importance of academic research that can enhance the effectiveness of sales training. Appropriate academic research that is effectively communicated to sales management has the potential to increase the efficiency of an organization's sales training program. Scant research has been conducted regarding the research needs of corporate sales trainers and sales managers who are responsible for sales training in their organizations. Research has indicated training executives believe that research published in academic journals is useful. Seventy-seven percent stated that academic publications were very informative, or of some value[21].

Sales training executives want future research to help them better understand their customers, the sales process, and how to treat clients after the sale is made[22]. The profession of selling has undergone a metamorphic shift in many aspects. Traditional selling practices focused on the short-term. Make the sale today. Salespeople directed their presentation towards their goals and needs. Specifically towards making commission on the transaction, and getting closer to achieving and surpassing their quota.

Traditional salespeople felt that they were the most important element of the equation. That is not so today. Professional salespeople view their relationship with their customers as a long-term relationship. If you do not make the sale today, there is always tomorrow. The direction of the presentation is not based on talking by the salesperson, but on listening to the customer. Today selling must be viewed as a solution to the customer's problem. Satisfying the customer's pressing needs. This mentality enhances a long-term relationship with customers. Post-purchase behavior, or measuring a customer's level of cognitive dissonance has become an important element of the sales process.

This shift has prompted a change in the delivery and content of sales training. Traditionally, learning, in the context of sales training, was directed at learning your products, and learning how to sell your products. The learning was product related, and the goal of learning was to teach you how to sell your products to maximize commission opportunities and surpass your quota. The content of learning in training programs needs be focused on the behavior of the customer. Learning should not be product focused, but customer focused. If you are trained how to think like the customer, you might actually buy into one of your own sales pitches.

Sales Training and Sales Development Conclusions

Sales training is often looked at as an elixir to cure problems within the sales side of a company. When sales are stagnant, and market share is slipping, the company's stock price is headed in the wrong direction, often a solution to the problem is additional sales training. An easy excuse when marketing plans do not meet corporate expectations is to state that the organization's salespeople need to be trained to solve the problem. The solution to these problems often have nothing to do with the training of salespeople, and are more related to other marketing, research and development, manufacturing, and competitive issues. No simple recipe exists for an effective training curriculum, but to further extend the medicinal metaphor, there are certainly symptoms of failure that can be easily diagnosed.

Everyone in the organization must be on the same page. The goals and directions of sales management must reflect the goals and objectives of sales training. If the goal of the organization is to achieve an established quota, and the goal of sales training is to train salespeople on how to sell a new but unproven product, a conflict of interest and direction can occur. Picture yourself as that salesperson where you are receiving conflicting directions from different segments of the organization. If you are encountering pressing customer issues in the field, and the sales training that is being delivered does not answer these needs, buy in from salespeople is difficult to accomplish. Sales training content needs to be a reaction to customer related issues in the field.

If a sales training program faces one or more of these problems, it will need to retool before it can be effective. Salespeople can benefit from new skills and knowledge. The solution is to take more time to look at the assumptions, methods, and outcomes of the sales training program, and make sure that the ends meet the needs of the salespeople.

As a salesperson matures, their self-concept moves from that of a dependent personality toward one of a self-directed human being[23]. As a salesperson's level of experience increases, and they become more mature with regards to their approach to how they sell their products, are self-directed sales training programs more efficient than traditional sales training curricula, which provide a traditional pedagogical approach to sales training? The pedagogical approach focuses on the practices of sales training in general and not on the needs of the sales trainee. Can self-directed learning initiatives have an impact on the effectiveness and efficiency of sales training programs? Self-study can further be defined as any method of study utilizing a self-directed approach. Self-study imposes more information knowledge than skill development. Salespeople, as adult learners, can respond to self-directed formats for sales training.

Selling is an entrepreneurial endeavor. In order to achieve success in selling, the individual must be self-motivated. Successful selling requires a proactive mentality rather than a reactive mentality. A self-motivated salesperson is a self-directed salesperson. A self-directed salesperson places the burden of learning on themselves, and a self-directed salesperson is very critical of their own performance, often placing performance expectations beyond those of sales management.

Research has established that salespeople have two divergent objectives: learning and performance. Some salespeople have an agenda slanted towards learning their products, customers, market, and industry. Other salespeople are driven by performance, where sales quota achievement takes priority over learning. A performance orientation is likely to lead to short-term payoffs, such as improved sales, whereas a learning orientation is likely to enhance skills and abilities that lead to better long-term performance. In a performance based environment success is in terms of today, immediate gratification and results. A learning orientation is more gradual. A learning orientation recommends self-directed solutions to problems that can develop a salesperson's selling ability and cognition, which can lead to improved levels of quota achievement. A learning orientation encourages salespeople to work hard, presumably because they enjoy their work, which thus leads to higher performance. Salespeople with a learning orientation tend to adapt their responses to selling situations and therefore perform at a higher level[24].

Research findings suggest that sales training resources for experienced salespeople be channeled towards a strategy that is more conducive to a learning environment that is beneficial to experienced salespeople[25]. Sales training for experienced salespeople should be focused on specific goals, for example, how to displace a competitor. Creating an optimal sales training environment for salespeople includes connecting the desired material with the current business plan that has been put in place by sales management. It is the obligation of tenured salespeople to suggest areas of improvement of the sales training initiative. This recommendation can be problematic because you are asking experienced salespeople to expose areas of their body of work that need improvement.

Effective sales organizations allow a field sales person to develop their own style of selling. As the salesperson's career progresses the individual's naivety can turn to cynicism. This cynicism is rooted in the redundancy and rhetoric that is put forth by the organization. Training the experienced, but cynical salesperson, can become a challenge. Experienced salespeople develop a cynicism towards sales training because of the redundancy of the message that the desired sales training is attempting to deliver. It is more of the same corporate rhetoric that they have heard before. Due to the repetitive nature of pedagogical sales training, salespeople view the endeavor as a waste of valuable selling time. The delivery of the sales training material cannot sound repetitive, but must sound fresh. In order to sound fresh, and have the experienced salesperson learn the desired material, one must explain how the desired sales training is going to impact their selling activity and put commission dollars in their pocket. Sales training and learning can be stagnated when the message does not connect to the current needs of the marketplace. Experienced salespeople are more in tune with current trends as opposed to less experienced salespeople who are more naïve. This disconnect coupled with the fact that sales training takes salespeople out of the field, can create an animosity towards the training content and they may perceive the exercise as a waste of valuable selling time.

Time management is an essential key to the success of a salesperson. Taking experienced salespeople out of the field can be a costly mistake. If a salesperson's time is being tied up in a rhetorical waste of time, the salesperson will not engage in the sales training initiative. Compensation is an effective motivator for salespeople. Engaging experienced salespeople in the desired sales training initiative, requires specifically pointing out how the additional sales training can have an impact on their selling objectives, paving the way towards exceeding their quotas and maximizing their commission opportunities. Experienced salespeople can act as an invaluable training resource to the organization. Tapping into this knowledge base can assist in the development of less experienced salespeople. This sharing of knowledge enhances the delivery of the desired sales training material when the less experienced salesperson hears the explanation from an experienced peer.

There is a need for a facelift within the discipline of sales training and sales development. Recognizing that business is an ever changing dynamic, means that the way that salespeople were trained yesterday, should not dictate the way that salespeople should be trained today and tomorrow. Once a sales training program is established, it must constantly change over time to meet the current trends in the marketplace. Sales training programs and sales training curricula should not be written in stone, they should be written in sand, and be more fluid and looked at as more of a work in progress. Evaluations of sales training programs should constitute the change. If proper evaluations are conducted, the shifts in the discipline should resemble a wrinkle, and not a complete paradigm shift.

We have become a win now society, with less grooming, less nurturing, less development, and more of an emphasis on immediate results. Sales training used to be a gradual exercise, where an individual is exposed to some initial form of sales training, and then released into the field, with some follow-up sales training done down the road. The benefit of this approach was to introduce the sales trainee to the fundamental basics, then send the sales trainee into the field for some beneficial "on-the-job" experience. The sales trainee was then brought back into an "off-the-job" environment where their "on-the-job" experience can be connected into the curriculum that the organization has put in place. Sales training is being frontloaded today. The learning curve has been accelerated. Today's frontloaded approach is to insure that when the sales trainee exits the sales training program they have an instant impact in the field, hence the need for more of a self-directed approach to sales training.

The bottom line is that your company can have the most extensive and expensive sales training program in your industry or known to mankind. It comes down to the individual and it is up to the individual to make the most of the sales training that has been provided. The purpose of sales training and sales development is to improve your skills as a sales professional. It is all for your benefit, but you need to take ownership of the resources that have been provided to you. If you capitalize on this opportunity you will become a better sales professional which can lead to increased commission dollars and give you the opportunity to maximize the financial goals and aspirations that you have set for yourself when you made the decision to pursue a career in sales.

The most successful salespeople are not necessarily the most experienced salespeople, but they are self-directed and self-motivated to achieve. The best salespeople are those who embrace their own sales training regimen. A self-directed salesperson takes the initiative upon themselves to go the extra distance to improve their performance. The self-directed salesperson is critical of their own performance, and is constantly reviewing their daily activity, to see how can they improve their performance.

As mentioned earlier, sales training and sales development is a mentality and a commitment, but not only from your company but from you the individual. You have to make a commitment to yourself that you will develop yourself into a better, polished, professional salesperson. Develop yourself, do not rely on your company for professional development, they might provide the vehicle that leads to professional development but it must come from you. If that means spending time in the evening reading and researching product manuals, or competitive products, industry issues, and market trends, so be it. It may require attending commercial sales training seminars, or enrolling in a graduate school course at a local university on personal selling, reading books on sales, subscribing to sales newsletters, reading blogs on personal selling, or joining sales trade associations. Whatever the method of professional development, you need to be proactive in your own development. As a salesperson you have to think of yourself as a sponge that needs to soak up as much information that you can, to become the resource, advisor, and consultant that your customer maybe looking for.

Chapter 7

Ethical Behavior in Sales: The First Thing That You are Selling is Your Integrity

The profession of selling has evolved from the traditional practice of transaction comes first, towards the development of a long-term relationship with your customer. Ethical behavior is the foundation of relationship selling. In following this evolution the question of ethics becomes more prevalent. If a salesperson is attempting to develop a long-term relationship with their customer, they must act and treat the customer in an ethical fashion. This paradigm shift in sales force behavior has raised the bar for ethics training, specifically for field salespeople. Salespeople need to improve their moral reasoning skills (ethical behavior) especially because customer impressions of salespeople generally recommend better ethical treatment.

Cognitive moral development reflects moral reasoning in the way individuals develop, over time, an increasingly accurate view and understanding of the nature of moral obligations in complex social systems[26]. A cognitive moral development approach to ethics training provide individuals with skills to reason through ethically troublesome situations and they are considered more effective than training methods that review complicated rules and regulations provided by some codes of ethics[27].

The question is that can a salesperson's level of cognitive moral development be increased through training? Research conclusions state that moral reasoning can be influenced through cognitive moral development training. The success of this approach points to replication of the actual selling environment. By recreation of the actual selling environment through the utilization of vestibule training (simulation), and role playing situations, the salesperson can be more prepared to act in a more ethical manner. As a salesperson becomes more experienced, their commitment to ethical behavior should increase.

Ethical behavior has always been an issue with salespeople. Salespeople have nobody to blame but themselves for the negative perception in the minds of customers. Everyone has been taken advantage of by a salesperson at some time in their life. Today's front page headlines have been filled with unethical behavior by other individuals who have nothing to do with sales, including CEO's, accountants, research and development, manufacturing, and politicians. The spotlight on unethical behavior now shines on everyone in the corporate structure and not just salespeople.

Ethics are an individual's own interpretation of a moral situation. You can make a statement that to some can seem like a horrible situation, while others dismiss it under the category of "that's just business." There is a huge delineation between unethical behavior and illegal behavior. Unethical behavior, while it might be immoral, and in so many words, not nice, it may not be against the law. Illegal behavior crosses over the line and can come with severe consequences.

What is an Ethical Dilemma?

An ethical dilemma exists when a salesperson is placed in a situation where they have to make a decision; do they do what is the right thing for the customer, the company, or the salesperson? There are advantages and disadvantages of serving the needs of all three stakeholders. What if the customer is ignorant to the situation, what if the company is ignorant to the situation? It is an interesting question to ask. The solution is what is the best long-term solution that maintains the integrity of the salesperson and preserves and cultivates the relationship between the salesperson and the customer? The first thing that any salesperson is selling when they walk in the door is their integrity. Customers buy from salespeople that they like. The second that your reputation, credibility, or integrity is compromised because of an unethical activity, is the second that you are finished in the mind of a customer. A salesperson can move from company to company within a specific industry. While today a salesperson is representing one company, tomorrow you can be representing another company, including your fiercest competitor.

There is a fine line that salespeople walk with regards to the pricing that they extend to their customers. Do all customers receive the same price? Is it unethical to charge different customers different prices on the same product? Is it unethical to bundle or tie in sales of products? A salesperson has two products, product "A" and product "B". The customer wants product "A" but only at a specific price. The salesperson counters with, "I can give you the price that you want on product "A", but you have to purchase product "B" as well." Is it unethical to do that? The ethical salesperson thinks so, the unethical salesperson shrugs it off as a necessary part of doing business. The point is that it is an individual's own moral interpretation of a situation. It comes down to a combination of the character of the salesperson and the training and ethical position that the company stands for that can help the salesperson solve the ethical dilemma.

Companies and salespeople exist and hang out on the unethical side of the table all day, because as long as they are not breaking the law, it is a necessary evil that is justified as a part of doing business. Unethical salespeople pass it off on the customer, who should know better, or if you will, have the awareness of buyer beware. It is never the unethical salesperson who is at fault, the customer should have known better.

Why would a company or salesperson partake in unethical sales practices? Competition is partially to blame. What if you do not have the best product, or work for the best company, or literally do not have the best solution to a customer's problem? The quota clock is ticking, and you need to make your quota, so it becomes easier to stretch the truth. Management is also culpable. Companies and sales managers that know that they are facing stiff, legitimate competition will train their salespeople how to act unethically. If your sales manager states that they do not care what you say in front of a customer, you need to make your quota, they are opening the door for unethical behavior to creep in. The salesperson, who wants to please the wishes of their sales manager, knows that in the eyes of their sales manager, this type of behavior will be tolerated and making the sale is paramount.

As a contrast, we have the sales management position, who from the first day of sales training, spews the company line that unethical behavior will not be tolerated and will lead to an immediate dismissal. When a sales manager states that they do not care what you say in front of a customer, if it is not factual and truthful, and if that means that you have to walk away from a potential sale, so be it. If you have to stretch the truth, it will not be tolerated. It is a mentality that must be dictated from the top down throughout the organization, that unethical behavior is not a part of how they do business. If this philosophy becomes ingrained in a corporate culture then the salesperson will not engage in the unethical activity.

Unethical behavior can be subtle and hard to detect. A salesperson is going through a routine sales presentation. A presentation that is duplicated all day, every day. As an experienced salesperson you can sense where the conversation is going, based on the body language and questions that your customer can raise during your presentation. There are two types of questions that can be raised, a great question, that gets you closer to closing the sale, and a problematic question that drives you away from making a sale. To the customer it is just a question, to the salesperson it is a great question and an awful question. If the customer raises the great question you can respond with a statement that gets the salesperson closer to closing the sale. What if they raise the problematic question? How do you respond? Do you spin the question; evade the question, or simply distract the customer? Is it unethical to do that? That is how subtle the line between ethical and unethical behavior can be. If you spin the question, or distract the customer the customer might forget about the question, remember to them it is only a question. How do you spin a problematic question, focus on a product feature. How do you distract a customer, ask them how was their weekend, what are they doing this weekend? The unethical salesperson believes that it is the responsibility of the customer to bring the conversation back to the question that they raised. They might never raise the question again, until it is too late when they purchase the product, only to find out that it cannot perform the way it was anticipated. The customer can doubt themselves by asking, "Did I bring this up during the presentation?"

As a salesperson, the majority of your time spent in the field you are alone, face-to-face with a customer is well over ninety percent of your time. Meaning that for the most part you are alone and do not have your sales manager or corporate compliance officer looking over your shoulder insuring that everything that you say about your product or company is truthful.

The end of a quota period is approaching, you are behind on your quota. A customer asks you to take an inventory of their current stock, and fill in a replacement order of where they are shy on their inventory. The customer is having a busy day, so they trust your judgment and let you fill in the order appropriately. Again, you are behind on your quota, and you need to get over the quota hurdle. Padding an order in sales means that you inflate the actual quantity that the customer needs to assist the salesperson in achieving their quota objective. Do you pad the order? Your sales manager does not know that you are padding the order. For the most part the customer does not realize that you are padding their order. The customer might not realize that you padded the order for months when they take a look at their inventory and cannot understand why they have so much excessive inventory on their hands. This is a consequence of padding, which can hamper your future relationship with your customer when they realize that you loaded them up with inventory. This can compromise the trust between a salesperson and customer and force the customer to never grant you the opportunity to place an order again for them without their approval. This can also stagnate future sales. What if that customer uses a certain amount of your product each month, almost like clockwork, but now they are overloaded on their stock so they will not be placing an order until their inventory is depleted. What if the customer has an unpredictable run of usage on your product and they do not ever realize that you padded the order? The question is, should you pad an order? It is an interesting ethical dilemma.

Sandbagging an order is the opposite of padding an order. Sandbagging occurs when a salesperson holds onto an order and does not place the order when it is received. Why would a salesperson sandbag, or to use another term, palm an order? Palming an order means that you have received the order but do not inform your company that you have received it and are keeping the order under the palm of your hand. Why would a salesperson do this? Is it unethical to sandbag or palm an order? What if the salesperson has either exceeded the quota, or has no chance of making the quota for the assigned period. This sale may have no impact on the commission that is earned for the quota period. What if it is advantageous to the salesperson to start the next quota period off to a good start? What if the percentage of commission is increased in the next quota period, where the exact same sale yields more commission? What is the harm in delaying the placing of an order a few days into the new quota period? Sales management will never approve of this policy, they want every order placed and shipped to the customer as soon as possible. Is it unethical to sandbag or palm a sales order? It is another interesting ethical dilemma.

Unethical Behavior Between a Salesperson and Their Company

Ethical behavior does not only pertain to the relationship between the salesperson and the customer, what about the ethical relationship between a salesperson and their company. Is it ethical for a company to hold back production of a product that creates a backorder situation, where an order is placed but cannot be shipped or processed because the product is not available? The job of a salesperson is to get the customer to say, yes, "I will take it." It is not the responsibility of the salesperson to have the product ready and available for shipping, when the sale is recorded. If an order is placed before the end of a quota period, and cannot be shipped and recorded as a sale, where the salesperson can miss out on making their quota, why should sandbagging or palming of an order be abhorred by sales management?

Is it unethical for a company to only care about shipping a product off of its loading dock and out of its distribution center, and not be concerned if the proper salesperson receives credit for the sale? Tracking and tracing of shipments is not as easy as it sounds, even with today's technology, it can be time consuming and expensive. The end result is that the wrong salesperson gets paid commission on a sale that they have no business making commission on. What about the regional sales manager who is involved, is it unethical for them to let this activity fall by the wayside, both territories might fall under their geographical region, so they receive the sales credit. What about sales territories where the actual line of demarcation on the map intersects and there are distributors from one territory shipping products into other salespeople's territories. Is this unethical? It certainly is not fair, the corporate stance usually is that all of this evens out in the end. Most times it does not, and typically nothing gets done about it, and so you have to live with it. Companies wonder why salespeople might practice some unethical activities between themselves and the company. The manufacturing strategy of loading up the warehouse and eventually selling a product has gone by the wayside. Today, especially if you are a publicly traded company where your responsibility used to be to your customers, it may have shifted to a responsibility to other stakeholders, in this case your stockholders. Maintaining and increasing the stock price of a company has become number one on the list of priorities for a CEO and senior management. The job of today's CEO is not necessarily to serve the needs of the customer, employee, or in this case their salespeople. No one is saying that they have disregarded these stakeholders, but they have been pushed to the bottom of the list. What is at the top of the list is the company's stock price, and CEO's have become more beholden to their stockholders than to the aforementioned stakeholders.

That is how they get to keep their jobs. Keeping finished product in inventory does not look good on a balance sheet and can negatively affect a stock price. Cash on hand looks good on a balance sheet and can stabilize or boost a stock price. In the past a company would tie up cash to manufacture product and place it into inventory, today most companies have employed some form of Just-In-Time (JIT) manufacturing and delivery process where low levels of inventory are kept on hand and manufacturing is scaled down to an as needed basis. The result of this is an increase in back orders, the CEO does not care that you did not make your bonus due to the back order, their allegiance is to the stockholder and stock price.

What does this have to do with salespeople? What does this have to do with ethical behavior? Inventory levels are at a record low, even the most profitable companies are operating at bone dry inventory levels and rely on Just-In-Time delivery systems where a product is manufactured on an as needed basis. What does this do for a stock price? Inventory is a bad word and ties up cash flow and can be a negative on a balance sheet and drive the stock price of a product down. Cash on hand can enhance a stock price, so many CEO's are placing less inventory into finished goods and are keeping more cash on hand. This can cause a back order, the worst nightmare for a salesperson. A salesperson is not on the manufacturing side of the company, you have no control over the manufacturing of your company's product. It has to be a two-way street otherwise the door has been opened for unethical behavior between the salesperson and the company. If a salesperson loses out on a commission opportunity because of a back order then a company should not be surprised when salespeople sandbag or palm orders to maximize a commission opportunity on the next quota period.

Ethical Behavior and Compensation Plans

A prescription to curtail unethical behavior among salespeople is rooted in the compensation plan that the salesperson works under. Straight commission plans, where the salesperson is only compensated after a sale is consummated allows the salesperson the grandest opportunity to treat a customer unethically. The contrary compensation plan, straight salary, where compensation is earned regardless of the outcome of a sales opportunity, can cause the salesperson to act in a more ethical manner. There is a sliding scale, and a happy medium that must be achieved somewhere between straight commission and straight salary. Many companies have adopted some form of combination compensation plan that utilizes an amalgamation of salary plus commission. If there is a tendency towards unethical behavior the scale needs to slide towards straight salary, if there is less of a temptation towards unethical behavior the scale can slide towards straight commission. Being on the extreme end of either side of the scale can be problematic. Straight commission opens the door for unethical activity because if there is no sale the salesperson can literally starve. Straight salary comes with the challenge of motivating the salesperson to make the sale when they are being compensated regardless if the customer says yes or no.

Many companies take the advantages of each form of compensation and slide the scale towards the middle, eliminating the disadvantages of being on the extreme end of either compensation plan. The advantage is that a salary is provided eliminating the desperation of, "If I don't make this sale, I will not eat tonight" mentality. It allows the salesperson to walk away from a sales opportunity where their ethical behavior can be compromised. Salespeople are motivated by the commission that they can earn on top of their base salary eliminating the motivational issues associated with a straight salary compensation plan.

Is Entertainment and Gift Giving Unethical?

Entertaining customers and giving gifts to customers without question places the salesperson near the edge of a cliff with regards to unethical behavior. Is it unethical to entertain customers? Is it unethical to give a gift to a customer? As with many elements in life it is all about moderation. Moderate entertainment and moderate gift giving are acceptable, excessive entertainment and excessive gift giving crosses over the line. What is the difference between moderate entertainment and excessive entertainment? Sporting events have long been a great opportunity to entertain customers. Taking a customer to a football game is moderate entertainment, which is still expensive. Taking a customer to the Super Bowl, paying for tickets, hotel, meals, and airfare is excessive entertainment. There has been a price tag placed on gift giving as well, around twenty-five dollars. That is an extremely moderate gift giving policy which results to a gift being nothing more nominal that a coffee mug that the customer can place on their desk.

The federal government and companies have started to place entertainment and gift giving under the microscope. From a legal standpoint is the entertainment or gift received a form of compensation? Who is at fault for this crackdown on entertainment and gift giving? Yes, salespeople, and sales management are to blame, some who have deep pockets when it comes to the discretion of an expense account. Some salespeople are actually evaluated on the use or nonuse of their expense account. If the allotted budget for entertainment is not exhausted, this can be a signal that the salesperson is not utilizing all of the company resources that are made available to them to maximize their relationships with customers.

Do not excuse the other person who is in the equation, the customer. There is plenty of blame for this unethical behavior on their side as well. Their hands are full of blood. What do you do as a salesperson when a customer puts their hand out and asks you, "What's in it for me?" The customer has abused this privilege as well. Customers are not naïve, they know that salespeople have expense accounts, and how unethical is it for a customer to take advantage of a salesperson's generosity by accepting an invitation for lunch, dinner, or some other form of entertainment when the customer has absolutely no interest in the salesperson's product. Bribe is a bad word that makes the ethical salesperson cringe. Ethical sales people have such an uphill battle to face on a daily basis, fighting the negative connotations associated with selling, that adding the word or concept of a bribe into the equation is a serious challenge that the ethical salesperson has to wrestle with. In certain parts of the world, bribing the customer is the start of a relationship, and the conversation does not move forward until this issue is resolved. The word value-added has replaced the word bribe, it is a much more softer phrase that can have the same meaning.

A solution to this unethical behavior is to put a policy in place that if you receive the excessive entertainment, or the excessive gift your job should be in jeopardy. If one side of the equation, the customer, stops putting their hand out soliciting the entertainment or gift giving, maybe it will be stopped, or at least curtailed and brought back to some form of moderation. Yes, a long-term relationship with your customer is recommended today, and clearly the environment for relationship development is enhanced in a restaurant, golf course, or sporting event as long as it does not become a gaudy, decadent activity. Thanking a customer for their business is one thing, being obligated to entertain a customer is another story. Once a salesperson starts the flow of gift giving and entertainment to a specific customer, it is hard to stop. The customer EXPECTS the gift, and can expect the entertainment. In the medical device and pharmaceutical industry it is common that a surgeon or physician will not give a salesperson the time of day until a luncheon or dinner is scheduled, for not only the clinician, but their staff and spouse. Regulations in the healthcare industry are now requiring that this practice be curbed to include only clinicians who are end users of the product. Education becomes the centerpiece of the entertainment and some portion of the entertainment must be focused on the education and training of the product to the end user, otherwise an unethical violation can occur. The unethical salesperson views the practice of entertainment and gift giving as a routine business occurrence, something that is part of the job. The ethical salesperson is not as comfortable with the entertainment and gift giving and is left with an empty feeling that they had to "buy" the business.

Is it Unethical to Disparage a Competitor?

The more competitive a selling situation, the more of a chance for unethical selling practices. Unethical salespeople spend most of their time in front of a customer disparaging their competitors. If a customer gives a salesperson thirty minutes of their valuable time and the salesperson spends twenty-eight of those minutes telling a customer what is wrong with their competitor's products, company, or salesperson, they have said nothing about their product, company, or themselves. Is it unethical to disparage, denigrate, or belittle a competitor during a sales presentation? This is a glaring signal that the customer is about to be taken advantage of by the unethical salesperson.

The unethical salesperson has said nothing about THEIR product, or THEIR company, or how THEIR product is a solution to customer's problem. Indirectly the unethical salesperson is sending a message to the customer, that they do not know what they are doing, that they are making a mistake if they choose the competitive offering. If they did know what they were doing, they would be purchasing the unethical salesperson's product. Especially, when a salesperson is trying to supplant a competitor, or convince and persuade the customer to switch from what they are currently purchasing to their product. The subliminal message is that, if you knew what you were doing, you would have purchased their product in the first place. The message is laced with inference that the customer is deficient when it comes to the ability to make the correct purchasing decision. How does the ethical salesperson dodge these competitive bullets and deflect these competitive arrows that have been slung their way? You should always acknowledge your competitor in a positive light, "They are a fine company, with fine products." Then you should acknowledge and respond to any objections that the customer has raised and then immediately focus on YOUR product, YOUR company, and how YOU can help solve their problem, with your product as the solution to their conundrum. A salesperson never knows where their career path can take them. A salesperson can end up working for the competitor that they have been disparaging, and now you are on their team. How does that enhance your credibility? The ethical sales person does the exact opposite of the unethical salesperson, they spend two minutes of their time during the presentation acknowledging their competitor, and twenty-eight minutes of the customers valuable time on their company, their product, and themselves.

By engaging in competitive disparagement the ethical salesperson is lowering their ethical standards to that of the unethical salesperson, with the result being a clouded and confused customer. It becomes a "they said, they said," argument leaving doubt in the customers mind as to who is really telling the truth? Stay professional, and do not compromise your integrity by engaging in this type of behavior.

Remember that customers can have a negative perception about salespeople and it becomes problematic to lump everyone together, the ethical salesperson needs to distance themselves from the unethical salesperson.

Ethical salespeople play by the rules that are put in place by the customer, unethical salespeople look for ways to circumvent the rules. How can the rules be circumvented? Let's say that the customer sets up a day when all of the members of the buying center (decision makers) are available for a committee presentation where all of the possible vendors show up to make a formal presentation and sales pitch. The customer states that they are on a tight schedule and every vendor will have sixty minutes, on the hour, to make their presentation and field questions from the committee. What does the ethical salesperson do if the unethical salesperson over extends their presentation and infringes on the ethical salespersons time in front of the committee? Is this just gamesmanship or an unethical act? The ethical salesperson now is left with a truncated time frame in front of the committee. What should you say? Why was my time compromised? Gamesmanship of this sort can be a subtle way for the unethical salesperson to nudge their way ahead of the ethical salesperson.

Ethical Conclusions and Recommendations

The professional, ethical salesperson is up front with all of the features and shortcomings of their product or company. What do you say if a customer asks a question about your product or company that can be construed as a negative? Tell the truth, "No, my product cannot function that way, or no, my company cannot extend the terms that you have requested, or meet the delivery date that you are requesting." Your response should be what your product and company CAN do, get the issue out there immediately. The ethical salesperson eliminates surprises after the sale is made. If that means that you have to walk away from a selling opportunity, so be it, then you were not the right match to solve the customer's problem. The customer will respect your candor and honesty, and you will leave with your integrity in hand, which can open the door for another sales opportunity down the road when your product is a better solution to the customer's problem. It all reverts back to the long-term relationship approach. If you stretch the truth eventually the customer will recognize this, and view your interaction with them as a short-term (transaction) approach, and you will never be granted a platform to introduce possible new product offerings in the future. Isn't it better to lose the battle today but win the war tomorrow? The unethical salesperson is consumed with the battle and not the war.

Solutions that can curb unethical sales force behavior have to emphasize the fact that unethical behavior will not be tolerated. Of course it all starts with leading by example, and ethical behavior starts at the top of an organization and can filter down and echo throughout the corporate structure. This can be accomplished by incorporating ethics training into the formal sales training program. Sandwiching in training sessions on ethical behavior in between product and selling skills training can enhance the overall sales training experience and break up the content that is being delivered. Codes of ethics or written company policies with regards to ethical behavior must be presented and displayed not only throughout sales training but on the company website, annual report, and product literature that is distributed to customers in the field. It must be a constant reminder to salespeople and something that is visible at every turn.

SECTION 4

Personal Selling Theory: The Science of Personal Selling

This section examines the academic theories of personal selling. It is designed to elevate the salesperson's acumen regarding the shift from the focus on the transaction to the emphasis on developing relationships with customers. To have a better understanding of who the customer is, and why customers purchase products. How to be systematic about your activity on a daily basis, and how to motivate the salesperson to achieve their personal and professional goals.

Chapter 8

Relationship Selling Versus Transaction Selling: Stop Worrying About the Transaction and Start Focusing on the Relationship

Traditional Transaction Selling Approach

The role of the salesperson is crucial to the overall success of an organization. Generating sales revenue and sustaining sales revenue were traditional roles. Current competitive trends in the industrial marketplace have rendered these roles increasingly less effective in establishing loyalty among buyers. There has been an underlying transfer in the theory and practice of corporate marketing. It has been suggested that we are in the midst of an ongoing paradigm shift in marketing from transaction marketing to long-term buyer-seller relationship marketing[28]. The role that the salesperson plays in establishing long-term loyalty among buyers needs to be redefined.

Traditionally, basic selling skills taught by sales trainers are based on models developed in the 1920's by E.K. Strong, who introduced such ideas as the use of open-ended and closed-ended questions, the presentation of features and benefits, objection handling methods, and closing techniques. Today these foundations for effective selling can still be utilized in formal sales training programs, with one obvious difference. These foundations are rooted in aggression and persuasion. These foundations were constructed during an era where straight commission was the primary form of salesperson compensation. This philosophy has bred a perception of deception, with regards to how salespeople treat potential customers. This is the transaction mentality. Relationship selling focuses on the long-term relationship between the salesperson and the customer. The prior foundations, which were rooted in aggression and persuasion, have been replaced with foundations rooted in empathy and ethics.

Established models of successful selling focused on the transaction itself. Completing the transaction and making the sale was paramount. Transaction selling concentrates on making the sale today, and is not concerned with tomorrow's relationship with the customer. It was a short-term approach to selling. Transactional relationships represent the traditional buyer-seller relationship. The underlying assumption is that value is maximized by an adversarial stance within the relationship where the buyer plays the suppliers against one another to extract a price or concession. These relationships are executed under market conditions with price being one of the most important variables[29]. Today that short-term approach has been replaced with a long-term relationship. The transaction approach focused on the close, while the relationship approach concentrates on the development of a partnership between buyer and seller.

Transaction selling emphasizes the wants of the salesperson, usually rooted in the commission that the salesperson can earn on the transaction. In relationship selling, the focal points are the needs of the customer. Relationship selling involves solving problems for customers, resulting in trust, which can enhance and lengthen the relationship. The buyer and seller working together in a co-operative non-adversarial way are at the heart of moving from transactional to facilitative and integrative relationships[30].

Definition of Relationship Selling Activities: The Birth of Relationship Selling

The concept of customer-oriented (relationship) selling was brought to the forefront in research conducted by Saxe and Weitz[31]. They defined customer-oriented selling as the degree to which salespeople practice the marketing concept by trying to help their customers make purchase decisions that will satisfy customer needs. Salespeople who are customer-oriented take actions aimed at increasing long-term customer satisfaction and avoid behaviors that may lead to customer dissatisfaction. Customer-oriented salespeople must take the necessary time and effort to identify unique customer needs and wants, and match them as closely as possible to the product benefits offering of the firm.

Instead of viewing selling as a series of struggles that the salesperson must win from a steady stream of prospects and customers of all sizes and shapes, relationship selling focuses on the building of mutual trust within the buyer-seller dyad with a delivery of anticipated, long-term, value-added benefits to buyers[32]. This popular philosophy calls for selling firms to abandon short-term transaction (individual sales) thinking and create long-term relationships, alliances, and collaborative arrangements with selected customers whenever possible[33].

Difference Between Relationship Selling Activities and Relationship Marketing

Numerous studies[34] proposed that relationship marketing refers to all marketing activities directed toward establishing, developing, and maintaining successful relational exchanges. Predominant among most definitions of relationship marketing is the view that buyer-seller encounters accumulate over time, and opportunities exist to transform individual and discrete transactions into relational partnerships[35]. This view supports the notion that a relationship exists when an individual exchange is assessed not in isolation, but as a continuation of past exchanges likely to continue into the future. One of the most important trends in sales and sales research has been the recognition that the long-term key to success may lie in a relational approach to the buyer-seller interaction[36].

Today, relationship marketing and selling are at the forefront of marketing practice and academic marketing research[37]. The theory of relationship marketing stems from its conceptualized positive effects on the nature and anticipation of continuous future interactions[38]. Directing marketing attention to existing customers to retain and enhance their patronage and loyalty through value-added benefits is becoming well integrated into the areas of industrial marketing and sales[39].

A formative idea in the development of relationship marketing thought states that there is a continuum of relational orientations[40]. The types of market relationships span a hierarchy from a discrete transaction to relational exchanges. A central theme to every market exchange is that value is given and received. Even in a short-lived relationship (transaction relationship), each side of the relational dyad gives something in return for a benefit or payoff[41].

Table #2: Difference Between Relationship Selling Activities and Relationship Marketing

Relationship Selling Activities	Relationship Marketing
Focuses on the needs of the customer	Focuses on the wants of the Marketing Dept.
Listening	Talking
Sales	Profit
Personal Image	Corporate Image

Relationship selling activities (See Table #2) focus on the needs of the customer while relationship marketing attempts to create a desire and a want in the marketplace. Relationship selling activities include the use of active listening skills, listening to the customer, to determine if the customer has a problem and a need for the salesperson's product. Relationship marketing is more concerned with getting the message out to the customer (talking) through the various forms of integrated marketing communications which include advertising, sales promotion, public relations, and publicity.

Salespeople are typically compensated based on the sales volume that is generated by their sales territory, while marketing executives are typically paid on the profitability of their product line. Relationship selling activities involve selling yourself to the customer before you sell your product. This includes presenting your personal image that can leave an indelible impression on a customer that can endure with the relationship between buyer and seller regardless of the company and product that the salesperson represents. Relationship marketing does have a long-term focus on the image that they portray to their customers, but it is more of a corporate image, not a personal one, that will generally outlast the salesperson's tenure with the organization.

Shift From Transaction Selling to Relationship Selling

Traditionally, the emphasis in sales was on closing (transaction) the sale, with little thought being given to the means by which the sale was obtained, customer expectations of the sales process, or the likelihood that any particular buyer would be a source of future business. Transaction marketing consists of single, discrete, exchange transactions where providers offer prospective customers goods or services for a fee[42]. Following completed transactions, the exchange relationship essentially ends.

Transaction marketing requires the availability of a mass market of willing, potential customers. Relationship marketing represents the opposite end of the hierarchy to transaction marketing. Thus, relationship marketing involves the establishment of an enduring, interdependent association between the buyer and seller. Relationship marketing necessitates that sellers become more knowledgeable about their customers' requirements and needs[43].

Despite the importance generally ascribed to the idea of exchange, marketing research has largely neglected the relationship aspect of buyer-seller behavior while tending to study transactions as discrete events. The lack of attention to antecedent conditions and processes for buyer-seller exchange relationships is a serious omission in the development of marketing knowledge.

The theoretical context that led to relationship marketing builds on differentiating relational exchange from discrete transactions[44]. The archetype of discrete transaction is manifested by money on one side and an easily measured commodity on the other. Relational exchange occurs when events are guided by the context of the interaction, including past, present and (expected) future experiences, and are different from discrete transactions, which are usually short-term events that are market driven. Organizational customers develop relationships with suppliers for a reason. They seek to receive benefits otherwise not available to them in purchasing from discrete transactions[45].

The difference between long-term (relationship) and short-term (transaction) oriented firms is that the first are concerned with achieving future goals, and both current and future outcomes, while the main concern of short-term oriented firms is current period opportunities and outcomes[46]. Another dissimilarity between the two selling philosophies is that long-term orientation is related to maximizing profits along several transactions, versus a single transaction in short-term oriented firms.

The emergence of the relationship-marketing paradigm in modern marketing thought consolidates the increasing importance given by marketing academics to managing, developing, and evaluating relationships[47]. Sales practitioners and academic researchers[48] have begun examining the importance and value of building relationships with customers. Current marketing trends recommend establishing long-term relationships with customers, fostering a customer-oriented selling approach among salespeople that is critical for developing long-term buyer-seller relationships[49].

Table #3: Comparing Relationship Selling versus Transaction Selling

Relationship	Transaction
Long-term	Short-term
Tomorrow	Today
Compensation Package	Straight Commission
Needs of the Customer	Needs of the Salesperson
Problem Solver	Pushy Salesperson
Integrity/Reputation Driven	Stretch the truth

Summary of the Differences Between Relationship Selling Versus Transaction Selling

The fundamental difference between transaction selling and relationship selling lies within the mindset of a short-term occurrence (transaction) versus a long-term association (relationship) between the salesperson and the customer. The role of a transaction salesperson is to stimulate, rather than satisfy the demand for their product[50]. To persuade customers that they need a supplier's product, salespeople in this role focus on achieving short-term results for their companies by using aggressive selling techniques to persuade customers to buy products. Transaction salespeople focus on today, and live for today. What can I sell today, how much commission can I make today, who can I take advantage of today, and are not concerned with tomorrow, or their future interactions (relationships) with their customers. If I do not continue to develop a relationship with this customer beyond this transaction, so be it, I made the sale today, I earned commission today, I completed the transaction. Transaction salespeople push (sell) the features of a product, while relationship oriented salespeople sell the benefits (solution) of a product to a customer.

Most treatments of relationship selling focus on the duration, rather than the creation, of a relationship which is typically defined as an orientation toward strong, enduring associations with individual accounts[51]. Relationship selling focuses more on the development of a connection between the salesperson and the customer, and relies on the enhancement of rapport building between both parties. Relationship selling is more concerned with tomorrow than today, if you are not ready today to make a purchase, or do not have a need for my product today, again, so be it, I will be there tomorrow when you are ready.

Traditionally, transaction salespeople were paid on straight commission, meaning that if you made a sale today, you earned a commission today. If you did not complete a transaction today, you did not earn any compensation for your efforts. Sales organizations have come to the realization that the commission earned on a transaction can affect the ethical behavior of a salesperson. If the salesperson's sole method of compensation is based on the transaction completed, this can have an effect on their behavior. While there are still many salespeople who are compensated on a straight commission basis, today it has become fashionable for salespeople to be paid a comprehensive compensation plan that includes the combination of a base salary, plus commission, bonuses, and related expenses. This type of compensation plan allows the salesperson to take the commission earned on the transaction out of the equation, or at least not forcing the salesperson to make the sale today because they need to make the sale today in order to receive any compensation for their efforts. It allows the salesperson to walk away from the transaction and not be empty handed because their base salary provides them with an income that does not hinge on completing the transaction.

Transaction salespeople are self-centered and direct their efforts towards their needs, specifically their need to make the sale and earn commission. Relationship selling requires the learning of new skills particularly in the areas of understanding customer needs and relationship development[52]. Relationship salespeople center on the needs of the customer, and act as detectives trying to uncover a need that the customer can have. If the customer has a need for a product, they have a problem. Relationship salespeople are perceived by their customers as problem solvers, compared to the pushy salesperson perception of traditional transaction oriented salespeople. Transaction salespeople stretch the truth, and try to fit square pegs into round holes. Relationship salespeople are more concerned with the integrity of the relationship, and their reputation as a professional, and fit square pegs into square holes.

Components of Relationship Selling Activities: Focusing on Customer Needs

Researchers outlined models of personal selling that described customer-oriented (relationship) selling. As opposed to the traditional sales-oriented (transaction) model of personal selling, this model emphasizes identifying customer needs and then matching them to the firm's offering. The researchers claimed that the main benefit of adopting a new model is that it will help to create more satisfied customers, but more importantly, helps build stronger interpersonal relationships with customers[53].

In an increasingly competitive and unpredictable business world, the ability to create and keep satisfied customers is the only route to long-term prosperity, which means that the role of personal selling must evolve from being sales-driven to customer-driven.

Components of Relationship Selling
Activities: Development of Partnerships

Relationship selling is an approach that focuses on forging long-term partnerships with customers. The goal of relationship selling is to earn the position of preferred supplier by developing trust in key accounts over a period of time[54]. Companies build relationships with customers by offering value and providing customer satisfaction. The longer customers are retained by a company, the more profitable they become because of increased purchases, reduced operating costs, referrals, price premiums, and reduced customer acquisition costs[55]. Companies benefit from repeat sales and referrals that lead to increases in sales, market share, and profits. Costs fall because it is less expensive to serve existing customers than to attract new ones.

Considerable attention has been given to the study of long-term buyer-seller relationships in marketing[56]. Firms are focusing considerable attention on building sustainable, competitive advantages by developing and maintaining close, cooperative relationships, with their salespeople playing a key role in the formation of long-term buyer-seller relationships. Researchers examined how the practice of personal selling and sales management is changing as a result of the increased emphasis on long-term buyer-seller relationships and to identify some implications of these changes.

Changes in traditional personal selling activities are needed to support the emergence of the partnering role for salespeople. For salespeople in the partnering role, the personal selling shifts from a focus on influencing buyer behavior to managing the conflict inherent in buyer-seller relationships[57]. The focus is on building relationships rather than making short-term sales. It is suggested that some issues concerning the emerging partnering role for salespeople deserve the consideration of scholars interested in personal selling research.

Components of Relationship Selling Activities: Thinking Like the Customer

The implementation of a relationship selling perspective requires a totally different approach from the traditional selling perspective. Relationship selling involves not just thinking about customers, but thinking like them. Reverse the role and see the sales proposal through the eyes of the customer. Creative salespeople focus on understanding the distinctive concerns of customers.

Relationship selling suggests a distinct technique of selling. It combines understanding customer needs, having a problem solving approach, and the creation of value through creative thinking. Salespeople play a critical role in helping to forge such relationships, as firms continue to adopt a customer-oriented perspective[58]. Further understanding of the relationship between the market-oriented, customer-driven firm and the customer orientation of the salesperson is needed.

Measures of Effectiveness of Relationship Selling Activities

Evidence suggests that long-term relationships can be achieved by having salespeople practice customer-oriented selling strategies rather than selling techniques directed toward immediate sales transactions[59]. In repeated exchanges typical of organizational purchasing, buyers may not only consider the cost and benefit pertaining to the single transaction at hand but also assess the cost and benefit associated with the formation and management of a long-term relationship[60]. Relational benefits and costs significantly influence the organizational buyer's perceived value, and these effects remained significant when compared to those of episodic antecedents.

Relationships Examined on the Effectiveness of Relationship Selling Activities: Trust and Commitment as Relationship Variables

Several scholars consider (Seller) commitment and (Buyer) trust as essential ingredients of long-term relationships[61]. Relationships involve cooperation, trust, mutual goals, interdependence, and social and structural bonding[62]. As a relationship deepens, communication becomes more open, trust expands and the partners become committed to make the cooperative relationship work. The notion of commitment importance in salesperson-customer relationships is not a novel concept. Commitment is the most common dependent variable used in buyer-seller relationship studies. Commitment as an implicit or explicit pledge of relational continuity between exchange partners. Thus, commitment implies importance, and a level of continuity to the relationship partners[63].

(Seller) Commitment is the motivation to maintain and lengthen the relationship. Commitment should be an important variable in determining successful relationships. Relationship commitment is a customer's enduring desire to continue a relationship with a seller accompanied by their willingness to make efforts at maintaining it[64]. Relationship commitment is central to relationship marketing. Relationship commitment exists only when the relationship is considered important; that is, the committed parties believe the relationship is worth working on to ensure that it endures indefinitely. Relationship commitment is considered vital because it is hypothesized to lead to cooperation, to reduce the temptation of attractive short-term alternatives, and to enhance profitability.

The level of relationship commitment distinguishes productive, effective relational exchanges from those that are unproductive and ineffective. One would expect that the level of benefits received from the relationship would be related strongly to both satisfaction with those benefits and satisfaction with the overall relationship.

Researchers presented a framework of relationship development that characterizes the process moving through four interrelated stages: awareness, exploration, expansion, and commitment[65]. A longer relationship implies a certain degree of commitment between the two parties. Relationship commitment represents the highest stage in relationship bonding.

Commitment among partners is seen as essential for each party in achieving its goals and for maintaining relationships. Customer perceptions of commitment are positively related to relationship quality. It is increasingly important that buyers have strong relationships with their suppliers to stay ahead of their competition. The establishment, development, and maintenance of relationships between exchange partners are crucial to achieving success.

A study considered two main sets of variables, interpersonal and relationship. Interpersonal variables describe the characteristics of individual company representatives, while relationship variables describe the nature of relationships between buyer and seller organizations. Relationship variables add an important dimension to the study of buyer-seller relationships. It is important for buyers to understand that their input is essential for developing and maintaining relationships and achieving cooperation. The study focused on the issues related to relationships from the buyer's perspective only. Findings recommended that because relationships involve more than one person, it is also important to look at the issues studied here from the salesperson's perspective. Looking at the salesperson's side of the story might provide further insight into why relationships between buyers and sellers are not always good and may suggest additional ways to improve them[66].

(Buyer) Trust is often cited as a critical component for determining relationship success[67]. What is the impact of behavioral, technological, and managerial forces upon personal selling and sales management? Research suggests that technology can never fully replace the salesperson's ability to establish trust with customers, respond to subtle cues, anticipate customer needs, provide personalized service, nurture ongoing relationships, and create profitable new business strategies in partnership with customers[68]. Much of the literature on customer relationships with a vendor firm's employees has focused on understanding the employee characteristics that contribute to strong customer relationships such as trust[69]. Trust has been defined as a customer's confident belief in a service provider's honesty towards the customer, and the belief that trust is the cornerstone of strategic partnerships[70].

Trust is broadly recognized as a positive element in working relationships. Trust enables cooperative behavior, promotes adaptive organizational forms, reduces conflict, and decreases transaction costs. Trust is so important to relational exchange because relationships characterized by trust are so highly valued that parties will desire to commit themselves to such relationships. Research results indicated that trust influences the way in which disagreements and arguments are perceived by exchange partners. When trust is present, parties will view such conflict as functional[71].

Trust is the belief that a party's word or promise is reliable and a party will fulfill their obligations in an exchange relationship. Trust is believed to alleviate risk and to increase cooperation in exchange relationships. Trust is central to the process of achieving cooperative problem solving and constructive dialogue, and also find trust to lead to higher levels of loyalty and commitment[72].

Trust exists when buyers and sellers believe that long-term idiosyncratic investments can be made with limited risk because both parties will refrain from using their power to renege on contracts or use a shift in circumstances to obtain profits in their favor. The results from a study indicated that buyers and sellers who perceived particular investments by their channel partners believed their partners to be trustworthy[73]. Trust exists when one party has confidence in an exchange partner's reliability and integrity, which is associated with qualities such as consistency, competency, honesty, fairness, responsibility, helpfulness, and benevolence[74]. When buyers perceive suppliers to be benevolent and consistent they become less worried about being taken advantage of by the suppliers.

Research found that buyer trust can be enhanced if the buyers perceive the suppliers to be trusting of the buyers, and if the buyers perceive the suppliers to be highly committed to the relationship[75]. Buyers' trust in suppliers is established when buyers believe in the suppliers' willingness to keep their promises and their ability to deliver competent and need-satisfying performance.

Trust reflects reliance on the other partner and involves uncertainty and vulnerability on the part of the trustor. Trust leads exchange partners to make risky decisions because they perceive the situation as having less uncertainty, rather than due to a global predisposition of the trustor to make any risky decisions. The supplier's willingness to commit time and resources and to stay engaged in the relationship will promote buyer trust. Continued resource commitments by the supplier can also enhance its capability to satisfy the changing needs of the buyer, further enhancing the buyer's trust[76].

Supplier commitment as perceived by the buyer does not serve to directly reduce buyer uncertainty. The supplier should continue to devote more time and resources to the exchange relationship with the buyer and demonstrate the spirit of dedication and commitment to the buyer, as these gestures would most likely enhance buyer trust, which will in turn reduce decision-making uncertainty. Buyer-perceived supplier commitment does have a significant, indirect effect on buyer decision-making uncertainty[77].

Buyer decision-making uncertainty can indeed be managed by building buyer trust, which in turn can be established by the supplier's increasing and demonstrating relationship commitment, trust, and dependence. A buyer-seller relationship based on trust and commitment does help to reduce buyer decision-making uncertainty. A buyer's trust in the supplier plays a pivotal role in reducing buyer decision making uncertainty. A buyer's trust in the supplier could be enhanced if buyers perceive the supplier to be trusting and committed to the business relationship.

As business marketers place greater emphasis on building long-term relationships, trust has assumed a central role in the development of marketing theory[78]. In accordance with the theory of trust and commitment, trust is considered a precursor of commitment. The logic behind why trust leads to commitment is centered on the current state of today's commodity driven marketplace where substitutes abound, and buyers have purchasing alternatives. Buyer trust must be a precursor to commitment. The relationship will not move forward without the trust of the buyer.

A major precursor of trust is communication, which can be defined broadly as the formal, as well as, informal sharing of meaningful and timely information between firms. Communication fosters trust by assisting in resolving disputes and aligning perceptions and expectations. The accumulation of trust leads to better communication[79]. An impediment to employees' motivation to share information was fear about how that information would be used. They also suggested that employees' trust in the firm is critical to motivate employees to share the information about their customers[80].

Identifying and modeling commitment and trust as key mediating variables is critical to the study and management of relationship marketing. If relationship commitment and trust were merely two more independent antecedents of important relationship outcomes, failing to include their efforts in studies of relationship marketing processes simply would result in less variance explained among the outcomes. However, as key mediating variables, failing to include their effects in such studies would result in flawed conclusions regarding not only the direct impact of relationship commitment and trust on important outcomes, but the impact of other antecedents as well.

Relationship trust and commitment are sentiments that have been identified as being critically important in the development of long-term firm relationships. Commitment and trust are key because they encourage marketers to work at preserving relationship investments by cooperating with exchange partners, resist attractive short-term alternatives in favor of the expected long-term benefits of staying with existing partners, and view potentially high-risk actions as being prudent because of the belief that partners will not act opportunistically. In short, commitment and trust lead directly to cooperative behaviors that are conducive to relationship marketing success[81].

Relationship marketing is powerful in theory but troubled in practice[82]. The relationship literature suggests that the future of buyer-seller relationships depends on the commitment made by the partners to the relationship, and that short-term sacrifices are normally necessary to realize long-term benefits. Because relationships characterized by trust are so highly valued, partners will desire to commit themselves to such relationships [83].

Importance of Salesperson Trust

Trust has been a focus of study across many disciplines including psychology, sociology, and economics. More recently, the concept of trust has received increased attention within management and marketing fields. One way trust has been viewed is as the perceived credibility and benevolence of a target of trust[84]. This conception of trust includes two components, objective credibility, or the extent upon which the relationship partner can be relied, and benevolence, or the extent to which one partner is concerned with the well-being of the other[85]. Marketing research on trust primarily focuses on two targets of trust: supplier firms and their salespeople. Trust of a supplier firm and trust of a supplier's salesperson, though related, represent different concepts. The salesperson is the primary contact with the buying firm providing valuable information and consultation to members of the buying center. To make current purchase decisions and long-term relational commitments, buyers must determine the extent to which they can trust their salespeople[86].

A sales force often plays a key role in interfacing with customers and implementing marketing strategy. However, as firms actively seek more collaborative relationships with customers, salespeople perform an important function in facilitating and developing customer trust[87]. When the customer's relationship to the vendor firm is weak and the relationship to the employee (salesperson) is strong, the greatest vulnerability lies in the firm's relationship with the customer[88]. The customer perceives the key contact employee (salesperson) as the critical value driver. Highly trusted salespeople can preserve customer commitment during difficult times created by management policies that appear contrary to the customer's best interests[89].

Organizational buyers who trust salespeople exhibit more integrative bargaining strategies, which leads to benefits for both parties[90]. Trust of an individual differs in nature from that of an organization. Understanding such differences is particularly important in business marketing situations in which the sales force plays a key role in implementing the supplier's marketing strategies and managing customer relationships[91].

Additional Relationship Selling Variables

Researchers discovered that the better the quality of the relationship, the greater amount of information sharing, communication quality, long-term orientation, and satisfaction with the relationship. Relationship quality (before, during, and after transactions) can build or destroy relationships[92].

Researchers investigated the moderating effects of the buying context on the relationship between communication elements and the effort buyers exert while searching for new suppliers throughout a buyer-seller relationship development process. The research examined four contingency variables: duration of the buyer-seller relationship, importance of a relationship to a supplier, size of a buying firm, and prior experience of an individual buyer. The researchers found that buyers would like to think that as relationships with suppliers progress towards long-term, mutual beneficial relationships, more quality communication with suppliers and less search effort on a buyer's part will be needed[93].

Studies on How to Promote Relationship Selling Activities in Sales Organizations

Researchers examined the effect of relationship selling activities on salesperson performance. A study explored the link between demographic selection criteria and the propensity of a salesperson to perform relationship selling behaviors. Research examining the effect of buyer-seller relationships on outcomes of the sales encounter has addressed several aspects of salesperson effectiveness[94].

Managers are faced with the challenge of implementing a relationship selling effort among their sales force. Unfortunately, many of the individuals comprising a given sales force are order-getters whose primary focus is transactional oriented. Researchers investigated the effect of generally accepted aspects of relationship selling on individual salesperson's satisfaction with their personal performance.

The research found that the existing sales literature generally agrees that customer-oriented selling leads to increased profits and customer satisfaction. Although most published sources state that customer-oriented selling is mandatory for the professional salesperson of the millennium, existing research does not empirically address the critical issue of the impact of one's customer-orientation upon that individual's satisfaction with their performance.

If salespeople do not believe that customer-oriented sales practices will positively affect their satisfaction with performance, they will be unlikely to engage in such practices for fear that they will suffer from sales declines. Thus, it is imperative that empirical research be conducted that examines issues regarding the customer-orientation and satisfaction with sales performance relationship[95].

Key findings of studies concluded that customer-oriented selling is positively related to performance[96]. Salespeople who practiced customer-oriented selling tend to be long-term relationship oriented[97]. Top performing salespeople tend to initially spend more time building relationships with buyers than attempting to gain a quick sale[98].

Little empirical research has examined the effectiveness of customer-oriented selling and the factors influencing the extent to which salespeople engage in it[99]. In many markets personal selling is a critical component of marketing success[100]. Yet despite an increasing amount of prescriptive marketing literature advocating a customer-oriented business approach, very little has been written about personal selling from a customer-oriented perspective. Personal selling literature lacks a comprehensive review that summarizes and organizes the empirical research regarding customer-oriented selling[101].

Both marketing and communication theory are in the midst of fundamental changes that are similar in origin, impact, and direction. The debates in communication studies and in marketing have arrived at the same conclusion: there should be less focus on functionalism and production, and more on relationships. Similarly, as the traditional marketing mix elements have become commoditized, companies are realizing that their most valuable assets are relationships with customers[102].

Understanding buyer behavior is instrumental to an appreciation of the relationship development process[103]. The seller's perspective (commitment) will require salespeople to look in the mirror at their own methods of relationship development with their customers. Researching this issue from the buyer's perspective (trust) will require salespeople to get inside the head of their customer, and force the salesperson to reverse the role, and think like the customer.

Today's long-term relationship selling approach focuses on the needs of the customer. Salespeople must have a problem solving style that portrays their motivation to the customer that they are there to help solve the customer's problem. When a customer needs a product, they have a problem. Salespeople today need their customers to view them as problem solvers, and partners in the process. In the transaction selling approach, customers perceive salespeople as adversaries, who only have their best interests in mind. This problem solving philosophy of selling has fashioned the need for this integrative model that combines all of the identified variables necessary to insure the development of long-term relationships between buyer and seller.

Communication between salespeople and customers, as with all members of society, has undergone a radical shift in today's information age. Salespeople are spending less time in face-to-face, physical interactions with customers, and more time in virtual interactions through the technological advancements of smart phones, laptops, tablets, voice mail, video conferencing, and electronic mail. This has enhanced the quality and efficiency of communication. There is less dependence on corporeal (physical) communication, but an increase in the notion that your customer can communicate with you as a salesperson, wherever and whenever the customer needs your assistance.

The transaction approach required the salesperson to be adept at leading the exchange of information. Transaction salespeople did most of the talking, exalting the benefits of their product. There was no formal sharing of information. There was limited dialogue. Transaction salespeople dictated to the customer how their product functioned and relied on persuasive and coercive selling tactics to convince the customer that buying their product was a wise and prudent decision. In today's relationship approach salespeople should sit back and listen, listen to the customer. Let the customer explain their situation and see if the customer has a need for your product. A need signifies a problem. Let the customer share the information regarding their situation, digest the facts given to the salesperson by the customer, and return with a solution to their problem.

The Commitment-Trust Theory theorized that the presence of relational commitment and trust are central to successful relationship marketing[104]. Marketing theory and practice need to make a paradigmatic shift towards developing relational exchanges. Successful relationship marketing requires relationship commitment and trust to be modeled as key mediating variables. The transaction method of selling does nothing to encourage customers to trust a salesperson. In fact, this approach does just the opposite, it discourages customers to trust salespeople. This relies on the fundamental fact that transaction salespeople have taken advantage of the customer, with a scope of trust that is limited to today's transaction. In the relationship approach trust must be earned before the relationship can continue. Once trust is earned and established, the relationship between buyer and seller is elevated to a higher echelon (commitment). At this point in the relationship the customer has reviewed their alternatives and has made the decision to commit to the salesperson and the relationship.

Long-term relationship orientation as a variable is more of a mentality that must be adopted not only by the salesperson, but by the customer. Both parties must come to the realization that a long-term approach is healthier for all parties involved. A partnership where both sides win, and where both sides sit on the same side of the negotiating table, instead of the transaction approach, which fostered confrontation, where both sides sat facing each other, each attempting to squeeze out a deal that was only in their best interests and was short-term in nature.

Once trust is established, and a commitment is made by both parties, it is important to be able to measure the performance promised by the salesperson. Did the salesperson deliver on the promises made during the evaluation process? Does the product perform as advertised? Is the customer satisfied? Satisfaction with the relationship must be measured to determine if the customer wants to continue with the relationship.

Chapter 9

Understanding the Customer: Who is the Customer and Why are They Buying Your Product?

There are two basic questions that need to be answered in sales, "Who is my customer and why are they buying my product?" It has become apparent that having a better understanding of the buying process and the behavior of customers can help the salesperson to be more successful. Getting inside the head of the customer and thinking like the customer can enhance the ability of a salesperson, especially their ability to analyze the selling situation that they are in the middle of.

Robinson, Faris, and Wind described the factors that affect the industrial (organizational) buying process[105]. The BUYING DECISION PROCESS includes all activities of organizational members as they define a buying situation, and identify, evaluate, and choose among alternative brands and suppliers[106]. These buying tasks that are performed in buying centers to solve the buying problem (what to buy, from whom to buy, when to buy, and in what quantity) are defined as five stages in that buying decision process:

1. Identification of need
2. Establishment of specifications
3. Identification of alternatives

4. Evaluation of alternatives
5. Selection of suppliers[107]

These buying tasks are further defined according to four dimensions:

1. The organizational purposed served: The reason for buying (e.g. to facilitate production, or for resale, or to be consumed in the performance of other organizational functions). Stages 1 and 2, (the need for the product and specifications) are related to the purpose served because when a buyer needs a product the buyer has a problem. The solution to the buyer's problem can be the seller's product. The severity of a problem has a direct influence on who gets involved in the decision making process.

2. The nature of demand: How the demand for the product is generated: by forces within the buying organization or by forces outside of the organization (that is, "derived" demand) as well as other characteristics of the demand pattern such as seasonal or cyclical fluctuations. Stages 1 and 2 (need and specification identification) are related to the nature of demand for the product because the product is the solution to the buyer's problem, thereby the nature of the demand for the product is related to the severity of the problem, thus creating the demand.

3. The extent of programming: The degree of routinization are stages, need, specification, alternative identification, evaluation of alternatives, and selection of suppliers are related to the degree of routinization. The more routine the decision, the less decision making authority required, the less time needed for identification and evaluation of alternatives, and less time needed to select a supplier.

4. The degree of centralization/decentralization: The extent to which buying authority has been delegated to operating levels in the organization. All stages, need, specification and alternative identification, evaluation of alternatives and selection of suppliers are related to the degree of centralization/

decentralization. The higher in the organization hierarchy, the greater the amount of decision making authority. The more authority is centralized, the higher the BUYCLASS, thereby casual decisions require less authority and the decision to purchase a strategic new product requires the most authority.

Buyclasses

In terms of programming or routinization, BUYCLASSES are: a Straight Rebuy, a Modified Rebuy, and a New Task[108]. These buyclasses are similar to those found in Howard and Sheth's description of buying decisions: Routinized Behavior (absence of problem-solving), therefore no search for alternatives: Limited Problem-Solving (limited search for alternatives); and Extensive Problem Solving (extensive search for alternatives)[109]. Note that by examining BUYCLASSES in terms of the description of the buying decision; the BUYCLASSES directly relate to the amount of time spent deciding on what to buy, from whom to buy, when to buy, and in what quantity.

Research advanced the BUYCLASS framework, and the classification of the amount of knowledge sought during the Buying Decision, and expanded three BUYCLASSES into six BUYCLASSES[110]. The revamped BUYCLASSES are: casual buy, routine low priority buy, simple modified rebuy, complex modified rebuy, judgmental new task, and strategic new task[111].

Casual Buy

The casual purchase is so named because the buying decision approach involves no effort to search for information, no analysis is performed, no consideration is given to proactive issues and much procedural control is applied. This approach is taken when the purchase is of minor importance, there is little uncertainty surrounding the purchase, many choices are available, and the buyer perceives that the buyer has little or no power in the situation.

Routine Low Priority

The routine low priority purchase is a more repetitive buying decision than the casual purchase (buy). The decision approach is to exert little effort to search for information, perform a moderate amount of analysis, only superficially consider proactive issues, and follow standard rules and procedures. Such buying decisions tend to be somewhat important, with a moderate level of uncertainty, many choices, and a moderate level of perceived buyer power.

Simple Modified Rebuy

The simple modified rebuy involves little uncertainty surrounding the purchase, a narrow set of choices, and a perception of moderate buying power. The approach is to do a moderate amount of searching for information, accompanied by a moderate amount of analysis, a high level of proactive focus, and a tendency to follow standard procedures.

Complex Modified Rebuy

The complex modified rebuy is characterized as quite important with little uncertainty, many choices, and a strong buying power position. The approach in this situation is distinct in its resemblance to the normative decision making model. Buyers use all the activities in a structured and seemingly rational process. The buyer searches for a great deal of information, applies sophisticated analysis techniques, give due consideration to long-term needs and supply, and closely follows established control mechanisms.

Judgmental New Task

A judgmental new task occurs when the firm is facing a great amount of uncertainty in the situation, a narrow set of choices, and moderate buying power. The approach is to do a moderate amount of search, analysis, and proactive focusing; but with little reliance on established procedures.

Strategic New Task

The strategic new task involves a moderate level of uncertainty and a narrow set of choices, and the buyer perceives a strong buying power position. The approach consists of a high level of search for information, a great deal of analysis, and intense focus on proactive issues; but with little reliance on established procedures. Though the approach is similar in pattern to that used for the judgmental new task, it involves much more effort on all the buying activities. The strategic new task is a distinct situation and decision approach because it involves the most important purchases to the firm, strategically and financially.

Buyclasses: Where is the Separation Between the Transaction Versus the Relationship?

The underlying rationale behind the success of transaction oriented selling is that the buyer is primarily interested in the best price for a commodity product. A commodity is a product that does not have any significant differences compared to its competitive products, and is sold strictly at the lowest price, where the seller earns a bare minimum (if any) profit. With commodity products, product differentiation is difficult. In terms of the casual buy BUYCLASS, and routine low priority purchase BUYCLASS; price of the product supersedes all other elements of the marketing mix, including the features and benefits of the product itself, the method of promotion, and the distribution strategy that the supplier employs, thus favoring transaction selling.

In an industry where there happens to be a myriad of competitive products and brands, where there is not much of a difference among the products, the transaction approach can be successful. These conditions lead to the conclusion that transaction oriented selling is the strategy that is followed when the buying situation is defined as a casual buy or routine low priority[112].

Conditions that favor relationship selling are different than the conditions that favor transaction selling. In relationship selling, the buyer is interested in more than just price. The buyer has questions about the features and functionality of the product. There are technical differences between products that need to be explained. The buyer needs to be trained on how to use and implement the seller's product. There needs to be an on-going relationship between the buyer and the seller due to product upgrades and enhancements. Since all of these conditions contribute to the success of relationship selling, these conditions lead to the conclusion that relationship selling is the strategy that is followed when the buying situation is defined as a simple modified rebuy, complex modified rebuy, judgmental new task, or a strategic new task[113].

Comparison of Buyclasses

Note that regardless of the type of good or service required and regardless of the BUYCLASS that business buyers follow: according to the decision-making model[114] the process to determine which vendor to use, the variance between the BUYCLASSES, is in the amount of time spent in searching for information. The search for information and the use of analytical techniques increase the time it takes to make a decision. The highest buyclass level, strategic new task, involves the most critical procurement decisions for a company. Often, when this decision is made, it becomes increasingly problematic to reverse the decision and then turn to a competitive alternative. These factors increase the time that it takes to make a decision, because once a decision has been made, it is a final decision. The search for information and the use of analytical techniques increase the time it takes to make a decision, because companies want to exhaust all available alternatives before making a crucial decision that has an overall impact on the performance of the company. This leads to the question, "What kinds of products are the best ones to sell?" Straight rebuy products, modified rebuy products, or new tasks? There are associated advantages and disadvantages of products that fall under each BUYCLASS category. It is common that an advantage of one BUYCLASS is a disadvantage of another BUYCLASS.

Table #4: Comparing BUYCLASSES Variables

BUYCLASS	Variable: Search for Information	Variable: Use of Analytical Techniques
Casual Buy	No Effort	No Analysis
Routine Low Priority	Little Effort	Moderate Analysis
Simple Modified Rebuy	Moderate Effort	Moderate Analysis
Complex Modified Rebuy	High Effort	High Analysis
Judgmental New Task	Moderate Effort	Moderate Analysis
Strategic New Task	Maximum Effort	Maximum Analysis

Straight Rebuy

The advantage of selling a straight rebuy (casual buy, routine low priority) product is that the buyer spends the least amount of time making the decision, it is a "no brainer." When a product runs out they simply reorder from the same vendor. The buyer does not have to solicit the approval of their supervisor to reorder the product. Straight rebuy sales are made all day every day. As a salesperson if you can build up a territory that is filled with straight rebuy customers, they can provide a steady stream of repeat business that can be the base or foundation of your territory's sales. Straight rebuy sales are consistent and predictable. Many times a straight rebuy sale is set up on a "blanket" purchase order. A blanket purchase order means that on a certain day of every month a shipment (sale) of products are sent to a customer. Today a blanket purchase order can be set up automatically and electronically where the salesperson does not even place the order but receives commission on the sale.

Straight rebuy products are the closest product in the BUYCLASS spectrum that sells itself. Straight rebuy products are the easiest products to sell, therefore the percentage of commission on straight rebuy products is very low. Companies know that straight rebuy products sell themselves, so they attach the lowest percentage of commission possible to the sale. The only way to significantly maximize the commission on straight rebuy products is to sell a huge volume of straight rebuy products. Some salespeople become bored with selling straight rebuy products, over time it is not as challenging as the other end of the spectrum (new task). It is the most routine of all of the BUYCLASSES, that routine over time can become stale and create an atmosphere that is not conducive for the motivation of salespeople.

Modified Rebuy

The term modified rebuy (simple modified rebuy, complex modified rebuy) means exactly what it says. Something in the buying situation needs to be "modified" or changed in the buying situation. It can be a quantity, a size, a color, something different from what is purchased in the straight rebuy BUYCLASS. Modified rebuy products are less commoditized than straight rebuy products which can open the door for competitive bidding. There can now be subtle differences between product alternatives which lengthen the sales cycle. Buyers must do more comparison shopping compared to the straight rebuy, a modified rebuy is not a "no brainer." Additional feedback from potential end users can be warranted. Although an initial relationship can be established between the salesperson and buyer during the straight rebuy, the modified rebuy gives the buyer the chance to solicit the landscape of competitive alternatives. This can keep the salesperson on their toes, knowing that the modified rebuy is a much more competitive situation than the straight rebuy.

New Task

The new task (judgmental new task, strategic new task) is the complete opposite end of the spectrum compared to the straight rebuy. New task sales are the most infrequent and in many cases will be less than ten in a given year. The fundamental difference between both ends of the spectrum is that a customer will have a need for your product in the very near future if you are selling straight rebuy products, as early as tomorrow. Once a customer makes a decision on a new task purchase it can be years, that is correct, years before they are in the market for your product again. Rejection is a daily occurrence in the life of a salesperson. Some salespeople deal with rejection better than others. As you become more experienced it becomes easier to live with. Rejection is not fun, rejection is not nice, having the door slammed in your face, the phone hung up on you, or simply being told to get lost is not fun. So the word NO becomes a bad word. Get used to the word NO if you are selling new task products. It is the opposite of the straight rebuy where you hear the words, "Yes, I will take it" every day.

Think about that, as outlined in a previous chapter on the psychology of selling, the mental side of a life in sales can wear on your psyche. Salespeople need to hear, "Yes, I will take it." It is music to the salesperson's ears, it is soothing, it is cathartic. Too much NO is not good. It is a big NO, it is a resounding NO! You need to have good days at work. You spend so much time working. A new task salesperson literally can have less than ten good days of work a year. That is not healthy, that is not enough, that lifestyle makes it difficult to get out of bed and go to work in the morning. It becomes a mentality of, "Why should I get out of bed, I am only going to hear No!, If I stay in bed I can't hear the word No."

The yes that you hear from making the straight rebuy sale is a tiny, miniscule, soft yes. At least it is a yes, and anything is better than the other alternative. By tiny, miniscule, and a softer yes, refers to the amount of commission that is earned on the straight rebuy sale. It goes beyond compensation, a salesperson needs to hear the word. The no that you hear during a straight rebuy sales situation is insignificant because you are around the corner from a yes, possibly on your very next sales call. Nothing compares to the YES that you hear when you close a new task sale. It is as resounding as the combination of all of the NO's that you hear and can be deafening, profound, and life changing. But life changing and profound does not mean that you have hit the lottery and you no longer have to work. It means that once that you have demonstrated that you can close the big deal, and possibly the sale of your life, you can have the confidence and perseverance to weather the storm in a life associated with being a new task salesperson.

A signal as to which BUYCLASS a product can fall under is the percentage of commission paid on each sale. A product that pays a commission in the low single digits as a percentage of commission slides more towards the straight rebuy, and is easier to sell. While a product that pays a double digit percentage of commission leans more towards the new task and is more difficult to sell, with the percentage of commission on modified rebuys somewhere in the middle. Sales jobs can also be classified in many ways, one way to separate the different types of sales jobs is to delineate the difference between a salesperson who is an order-taker versus a salesperson who is an order-getter.

Salespeople who are order-takers sell straight rebuy products and often show up for a sales presentation with the mentality of, "How many do you want today." Order-taking salespeople catch a bad rap. Anybody can be an order-taker, anybody can be trained to show up and take an order. Order-taking requires the least amount of selling skills and selling expertise, that is why the commission percentage that order-takers earn is low. It can be a fertile atmosphere that gives a salesperson an entree into the profession that can lead to more advanced sales jobs down the road. Order-getters are the most experienced and skilled salespeople. Order-getters earn the highest percentage of commission on the sales that they make. Order-getters sell new task products and are veteran, weathered salespeople who have mastered the art and science of selling and embrace the challenge of going after and getting an order.

Which is the best sales job to have, a straight rebuy, modified rebuy, or the new task? It is a trick question, but it really comes down to the individual salesperson. Salespeople who are new to sales or new to an industry or market can find that selling straight rebuy products are right for them because it can teach the salesperson the necessary skills needed to be successful at selling. Straight rebuy salespeople learn how to interact with customers, how to process sales orders, and other regimental activities that salespeople go through and face on a daily basis. The modified rebuy salesperson takes the experience that the salesperson has learned as a straight rebuy salesperson and takes it to the next level. The sales cycle and sales volume for modified rebuy salespeople is escalated and can enhance the motivation of the straight rebuy salesperson who has made the transition to the modified rebuy salesperson. The new task salesperson has the opportunity to maximize their compensation goals and aspirations but comes with a life that is associated with rejection. So which is the best sales job to have?

It can come down to your own personal situation. Demographic factors can influence what BUYCLASS products are right for an individual salesperson. What stage of life is the salesperson in, what is going on in their life that can have an impact on what type of compensation is the best for them? If you are young and new to sales maybe a straight rebuy job is beneficial. If you are single maybe the new task is more enticing. If you are married and have a family to support, the modified rebuy can be an attractive alternative. What if your spouse has a career with a steady paycheck, then maybe the salesperson can explore the new task opportunity. What if your spouse has a career where the compensation can vary, then maybe the salesperson should pursue the straight rebuy opportunity which allows for a more consistent flow of compensation. The point is that a career in sales can provide the flexibility in compensation that can be tailored to the salesperson's lifestyle.

Many companies have multiple product lines that they offer to the marketplace. It is common for a company to have some products that are straight rebuys, some that are modified rebuys, and some that are new tasks. The optimal sales job is the one that offers a combination of all of the BUYCLASSES. This combination can provide the necessary balance that a salesperson needs. A salesperson needs the affirmation associated with the straight rebuy, needs the middle road correlated with the modified rebuy, and needs the carrot that is connected with chase of the new task.

Over time selling on either extreme of the BUYCLASS continuum can lead to burnout or dissatisfaction with the current selling situation and cause the salesperson to seek new sales opportunities. The combination plan can accentuate the advantages of each BUYCLASS and minimize the shortcomings of each BUYCLASS. An excellent way to achieve the balance is to integrate the sales activity associated with each product BUYCLASS. Flexibility is the key. Some salespeople start the day fresh where they are more apt to be able to deal with the stress associated with rejection, so they can focus their sales call activity on new task sales opportunities. By the end of the day, after fighting rejection all day, can be a great time to make straight rebuy sales calls. Remember the little yes, that is associated with the straight rebuy sale. That little yes, can help soften the hard rejection received earlier in the day associated with making new task sales calls. Finish the day on a positive note. When reviewing the day's sales activity, at least it can be capped off on a positive note, and may help the salesperson sleep at night.

This analogy can be applied to any time frame and not just one day in the field as a salesperson. It can be applied weekly, where the salesperson chooses to make new task sales calls early in the week but wants to finish the week on an encouraging note, devoting their time on straight rebuy sales calls. It can be on a monthly basis, a quarterly basis, or even an annual basis, where a salesperson can spend the first half of an entire sales year setting up straight rebuy sales which can generate automatic blanket purchase orders, and then dedicate the balance of the sales year hunting down new task sales opportunities.

The real estate business mirrors the BUYCLASS model. A real estate office can have multiple product offerings including apartment rentals, mid-range homes for sale, and listings of high end mansions. Apartments are rented every day (straight rebuy), mid-range homes are sold every month (modified rebuy), and a few mansions (new task) are sold every year. While a real estate agent can specialize on one BUYCLASS over the other, doesn't it make sense to have some balance in your sales activity that can make for a more well-rounded real estate sales professional?

The surgical instrument business can follow this model as well. Hospitals place orders every day for scalpels and scissors (straight rebuy). Periodically there is a need to replace additional instruments. Surgical instruments are grouped by the type of surgical specialty and surgical procedure. For example, there are specific surgical instruments for heart surgery and different surgical instruments for hip surgery. All of these instruments are assembled in a set and placed in a tray or container. This container already houses the scissors and the scalpels, but once in a while there is a need to replace or purchase (modified rebuy) an additional set or tray which not only includes the scalpels and scissors, but can include needle holders, retractors, and other related bone cutting and flesh cutting instruments.

At the time that a hospital undergoes an expansion of surgical services can be the time for them to take a look at their overall inventory of all surgical instruments. This includes an analysis of how their inventory is being used, and what additional sets of instruments need to be purchased (new-task). Instead of replacing one set of instruments for a specific surgical specialty, ALL sets must be analyzed and a utilization of the inventory is conducted. This can reveal what inventory needs to be purchased to upgrade all of the surgical instruments used in the hospital. This is an incredibly time consuming exercise that can lead to a humungous sale (new task) but once the exercise is completed, another physical inventory is not necessary for several years.

Buying Center

Researchers have focused on the factors that affect buying center structure (organization) and functions (purchasing decisions) including the individual participants, interpersonal activities, sentiments, interactions, the organizational climate, and the environment. Research examined the influence of the purchase situation on the organization (structure) of the buying center. Findings included a strong association between the newness of the purchase and the amount of information desired by the decision-makers, the amount of information processed by the decision-makers, and the time spent making the decisions[115].

Robinson, Faris, and Wind concluded that the amalgamation of features of the buying situation are more important than the type of product (one of those features) in determining industrial buying behavior[116].

Webster and Wind contend that since the BUYCLASSES are defined by and influence the organizational buying process, BUYCLASSES must be considered in appraising market opportunities[117]. Marketing strategies must be adjusted according to the five stages in the decision process because different members of the buying center are involved, different decision criteria are employed, and different information sources become more or less relevant[118]. In terms of those information sources, models have been proposed that focus on when the seller should focus on the transaction (the sale) and when the seller should focus on the relationship between the buyer and the seller.

There are significant differences between selling products to consumers and selling products to businesses. The focus of this book, while it does have applications for selling products to consumers, is more tailored toward the business customer. Advantages of selling products to businesses are the volume of the sale, the repetitive nature of the sale (repeat business) and the ease of identifying the type of customer. Who makes the decision on what products to purchase? A rule of thumb is that the more money that is being spent on a buying decision, the more people who get involved in the buying decision. The more people who get involved in the buying decision, the more departments that get involved in the buying decision. The more departments that get involved in the buying decision the more time it will take to make a decision.

The decision making unit of an organization is known as the Buying Center[19]. The Buying Center includes all of the individuals and units that play a role in the purchase decision making process. This group includes the actual users of the product, those who make the buying decision, those who influence the buying decision, those who do the actual buying, and those who control the buying information. The buying center includes all members of the organization who play any of the roles in the purchase decision process.

Initiator:

An initiator is the first employee in an organization who recognizes a need for a product, brings it to the attention of the organization and is requesting that action to solve the problem be initiated.

Users:

The user is the employee who will actually use the product in their daily activity at work. The user is possibly the only employee who actually puts their hands on the product. Users can help design the product specifications and detail why a specific product is needed. A user can also be the initiator.

Influencers:

Influencers can stipulate the criteria that is used to evaluate alternatives. Influencers have the technical expertise to separate the features and benefits of the product alternatives that are being considered. They can be users of the product as well, but typically have more of a voice (influence) in the purchase decision.

Buyers:

The buyer's role in the buying center is to negotiate the terms of the purchase. The buyer also is the buying center member who facilitates the transaction, and actually places the order for the product.

Deciders:

The decider has the ceremonial status within the buying center to choose and endorse the vendor. The decider is the most difficult member of the buying center to make a sales presentation to, because they are important high level executives in the organization's hierarchy.

Gatekeepers:

The gatekeeper controls the flow of information to other members of the buying center. Purchasing agents often have authority to prevent salespeople from seeing users and deciders. Purchasing agents can view their gatekeeping role as the foundation of their power. Other gatekeepers can include technical personnel and personal secretaries. A secretary can act as a gatekeeper by deciding which vendors obtain an appointment with a buyer. Too often salespeople discount the power that the gatekeeper can have. They can wrongly assume that they do not have any power or influence on the decision to purchase a product. This is the furthest thing from the truth. The gatekeeper plays a major role in the buying center.

The buying center can vary from company to company and there can be multiple buying centers within an organization. It comes down to what problem is the company trying to solve with the purchase of a product acting as the solution to the problem. The buying center is not a formal department and does not show up on an organizational chart. It is more of a group of employees who get together to resolve an issue that the company is having. The more structured the organization the more structured the buying center. It often is organized by a committee format. With a chairperson and associated committee members who all play a different role in the buying center. The chairperson can be the decider, but the chairperson can also be the buyer or influencer. That is the problem, this is a fluid and dynamic group of customers, and a salesperson needs to ascertain who is in what role in the buying center. In one buying center the user can have more of a voice in the decision than another. In another buying center the buyer is really making the decision regardless of what the user says. A buying center can include noticeable departments that can be common between different companies but their role and their degree of influence can vary from company to company.

What can extend the sales cycle is the commitment by the buying center to convene as a group and make a decision. The problem is that all of the members of the buying center have THEIR regular job to do. They are busy, so carving out time for the buying center to get together can be a challenge. Some buying centers choose to meet on a specific day of the month, for this example the first Thursday of the month or the last Wednesday of the month. If they cannot come to a decision, the committee does not meet again until the next month and this can frustrate the salesperson. It comes down to a sense of urgency. How urgent is it that the buying center comes to a conclusion? Product alternatives need to be considered, possible product trials and evaluations have to take place. You as the salesperson may not be the only vendor that the customer is considering, kicking the can down the road when it comes to choosing a vendor.

Other pitfalls that salespeople face when dealing with the buying center is finding out who is really making the decision to purchase the product? Everyone has an ego and it is fashionable for a member of the buying center to say to a salesperson when it is just the two of them that, "I am very important in this company." This may be true, but maybe not as true as the customer thinks for this purchase decision. Who do you believe? Trust no one, assume that every member of the buying center has some influence on the purchasing decision. A tip to determine who is really calling the shots is to observe the buying center when you are in front of them as a committee. Where does the chairperson sit? At the end of the table, in the middle of the table? Observe how other members of the buying center defer to each other. This can be a signal as to who in the buying center regardless of their job title can have more influence over the group than others. A salesperson needs to have a champion in the room. A champion is a member of the buying center who will standup and exert their influence on the group. Again, a champion can be the user, influencer, or buyer. A champion sells the salesperson's product in front of the buying center when the salesperson leaves the room and only buying center members remain.

An issue that is out of the control of the salesperson is the political atmosphere among buying center co-workers. There can be conflicting political agendas and determining a consensus among buying center members is not as easy as it sounds. What if one member is in favor of one vendor for whatever reason, but another buying center member sides with a different vendor just to intentionally disagree with the other member? This is common and can impede the success of the salesperson.

The balance of power can shift from buying center to buying center. An example of how the same job title can have different roles in the buying center is a hospital. In some hospitals surgeons have the power to make the decision on what products to use, while in others nurses make product decisions. Still in others supply center managers can make the decision or buyers and hospital administrators can exert their influence. This can be different in another hospital that literally can be across the street. You can sell the same product for the same price to the same customer yet the individual pulling the trigger on the sale can vary from customer to customer.

Chapter 10

Steps in the Selling Process: The Importance of Moving Your Business Forward

To be successful in sales you have to be persistent, dedicated, and hard working. You need to be scientific in your approach, meaning you have to have a plan. You have to be robotic with your activity, every day you need to have a routine that identifies and follows steps that can lead you to success. You need to move your business forward every day, you need to accomplish something today that gets you closer to surpassing your quota.

The sales process can be defined as the steps that you need to follow from starting from scratch, or locating your potential customer, to approaching the customer, making a presentation to the customer, answering any questions or objections that they have, closing the sale, and following-up with the customer after the sale. If you follow these steps, and adhere to this model, you can be successful at selling. You need to know where you are going every day, you need to know where, and what stage of the sales process your customers are in. Every customer is at a different stage of the process, you need to be able to juggle this, know when to move to the next stage, and when to start the process over again with your next customer.

The sales cycle is the amount of time it takes from the first time you identify a potential customer to the time it takes to close the sale. It is the "A to Z" of selling. You need to know where you are in the sales cycle from "A to Z". Some sales cycles are short, some are longer. The more dollars that are at stake, the more departments that get involved in the process, the more departments that get involved in the process, the more people get involved in the process. The more people that get involved in the process, the longer it takes to close the sale. The key is to shorten the sales cycle. Salespeople who are able to move their business forward every day and shorten the sales cycle are the salespeople who consistently exceed their quota, and become super-star salespeople.

Prospecting

How do you get started? Where do you go? Who do you see? Some companies put you through their sales training program, release you into the field, and hand you the keys to the company car and say, "Go ahead, go get them!" Now, this is not necessarily such a bad thing, to be cut loose into your territory where you are in charge of where you go on a daily basis. You have to have a plan. It all starts with prospecting.

Prospecting dates back to the mid 1800's, during the gold rush, when prospectors headed west in search of their fortune. They were looking for precious bullion, standing in a river with a pan in their hand and searching for gold. That is exactly what you are doing when you start the sales process. You are on a quest to locate the precious bullion, in this case your customer. A prospect is a potential customer, but not all potential customers are prospects. There is a difference between a prospect and suspect. A prospect is a legitimate potential customer. A suspect is someone who is disguised as a prospect, who on the surface might seem to be a prospect, but in reality is really a suspect who is not going to buy your product and ends up wasting your valuable sales time. Something else that separates the prospects from the suspects is the magic formula. The magic formula is the combination of two ingredients that without the presence of both, can immediately move your prospect into the suspect file. The prospect has to have a need for your product, and have the ability to pay for your product. If they have the money but do not have a need then they are a suspect. If they have a need but cannot afford your product they also are a suspect. You need to spot the suspects and delineate them from your prospects and move forward with your approach.

There are several methods of prospecting. Which is the most effective form of prospecting? It is a trick question. The most effective method is the method that works for you. It is the method that you are most comfortable with. Make no mistake about it, you HAVE to prospect. You have to always be hunting and searching for new customers. The day that a salesperson wakes up and is comfortable with the amount of current, existing customers that they have in their territory, is the first day that the sales in your territory will slowly begin to erode away.

You need new customers, you need to infuse new blood and new business (customers) into your territory. You can have the most loyal customers in your territory that have helped you achieve your quota in the past. The only thing that you can count on in business is that things will change. The way that you do business today, is not the way that you did business yesterday. The way that you do business today will not be the way that you do business tomorrow. The same goes for your customers. Their needs can change. They might need your product today, but there is no guarantee that they will need your product tomorrow. Customers can move out of your territory, they can go out of business, or unfortunately pass away, and now the sales that they have been fueling your territory with, suddenly leave a hole in your quota that needs to be replaced.

Prospecting is not fun, closing the sale is fun. Prospecting is painful, closing the sale alleviates the pain associated with prospecting. If you do not prospect you will never get to closing the sale. Prospecting is not fun because it is filled with rejection. Having the phone hung up on you, having a door slammed in your face, having a prospect tell you to get lost is not fun. That is why you need to find the best method of prospecting that works for you. There is a helpless sense that you are wasting valuable sales time, because you will waste time prospecting. Remember the quota clock is always ticking, and a minute wasted by unproductive prospecting is a minute that could have been spent closing a sale.

Prospecting is a mentality, it is a grind, it is a necessary evil that must become part of your daily sales activity. Whatever works for you, whatever you are comfortable with will be how you establish your routine. Some salespeople prospect early in the day, to get it out of the way, some salespeople handle immediate, pressing sales and customer related issues first, and leave their prospecting for the end of the day. Some prospect earlier in the week, some wait until the end of the week. The same goes for a monthly basis, some salespeople prospect in the beginning of the month because they know that their time at the end of the month is more beneficial to be spent closing sales before the end of the month.

A method to alleviate the pain associated with prospecting is to sandwich your prospecting around solid appointments during the day, week, or month. Too much prospecting in a given time period can weigh on you psychologically. As you review your daily activity your day can be highlighted by the sales calls that did move your business forward, as opposed to a full day of prospecting that can leave you with a depressing, empty feeling that you were spinning your wheels all day and were not productive. Call reluctance can set in where you are doing too much prospecting and the rejection that you are experiencing can actually prevent you from making your next attempt at prospecting. A mentality exists where, "If I do not pick up the phone, they cannot hang up on me." Call reluctance can also exist in physical, face-to-face (door-to-door) prospecting. If you do not knock on the door they cannot slam the door in your face, or throw you out of their office or place of business. You have to fight through call reluctance, which is common and normal, but if you do not pick up the phone, or knock on that door you will never find any new customers. As you become more experienced you can handle the rejection associated with prospecting, and recognize that it is a part of the life that you have chosen as a salesperson, and you will develop a thicker skin that can help adjust to the rejection.

What is the right method of prospecting for you? You should use the method that works for you, but it is also recommended to use multiple methods because you can never predict where you will find your next prospect. It does not matter what method works for you, or how you found the customer, what matters is that you FOUND the customer! The easiest place to start is with account lists given to you by your company. They will provide you with a database of customers in your territory, and how much sales volume each account generates. Some accounts generate more revenue than others. You need to prioritize your time and decide who you should call on and who you should not.

Some company account lists might only list customers who have purchased something from your company in the past, so there can be other potential prospects in your territory. Technology is a wonderful tool, and today you can go to the Internet and search for all potential prospects in your geographical territory with a couple of clicks of a mouse. Let's say that in your territory there are fifty accounts that your company has identified as a customer who has purchased a product from your company in the past. Your search revealed that there are an additional fifty customers in your territory that have never purchased a product from your company. You can access their contact information and there you go, you now have a list of one hundred prospects that are potential customers.

Cold calling, where you attempt to contact a prospect "cold", with no previous knowledge of you, your company, or your product, is a method of prospecting that spurs a debate that must be addressed.

There is a feeling that you MUST endure some level of cold calling in your prospecting. The other end of the spectrum is that cold calling can be ineffective due to the time that is wasted utilizing this method of prospecting. There are other methods of prospecting that can be better utilizations of your time.

Sales is a numbers game and the more prospects that you ask to purchase your product the better your chances of someone saying, "Yes, I will take it!" If you ask one hundred prospects to purchase your product, you will have a chance of making a sale, but if you ask one thousand prospects to purchase your product your chances of making a sale will increase tenfold. It is common for salespeople to loathe or dread the concept of cold calling. Here is a tip, sales managers love the idea that their salespeople are cold calling. It shows initiative and dedication to the cause. Any salesperson can get an existing customer to re-order a company's product. The over achieving salesperson consistently cold calls and brings in new business from new customers. Yes, any sale regardless of size is considered a win. A sale that is consummated as a result of a cold call is a much sweeter victory. Sales is a roller coaster ride filled with highs and lows, and the high that you will experience from a "cold call" sale is one of the true enjoyments in the life of a salesperson. You did it, you germinated, and nurtured the process, you can take full credit for it, and this will go a long way with sales management.

Qualifying the prospect is a method of warming up the cold call. It can help you to be more productive with your cold calling. A qualified prospect is not just any potential customer, but a specific customer. Depending on the type of customer that they are, they can have more of a need for your product. An example can be that you sell products to hospitals. Are all of the hospitals in your territory prospects? On paper, yes, but in reality no. What if your product is a cutting edge technology, that is expensive? Not all of the prospects (hospitals) in your territory are interested in the latest technology, or can afford the new technology. You need to do some homework and identify which prospects (hospitals) are interested in the latest and greatest technology, narrow down your list and then begin to cold call on them. Another example could be that your product is designed for a specific hospital specialty, in this example, cardiac surgery. A hospital is a hospital, but not all hospitals perform cardiac surgery. Your homework is to determine who does cardiac surgery and who does not. You can have one hundred hospitals in your territory, but through your research, which can be accomplished by visiting the website of all of the hospitals in your territory, you determine that thirty of your hospitals (prospects) perform cardiac surgery and seventy of your hospitals (suspects) do not. You now can focus your cold calling on the prospects identified and not waste your time on the suspects.

Another example is the financial services, or in this case, the life insurance industry. Forever, a technique of prospecting in this business has been to pick up the telephone and start dialing for dollars. Get the phone book and start with the letter "A" and start making phone calls to prospective customers. Remember, everyone is a potential customer for life insurance. If you make one thousand phone calls, in this case randomly, eventually someone is going to say yes. There is no rhyme and reason behind this method, it does work, but you can waste a tremendous amount of time. The same method of qualifying the prospect applies here. There are circumstances that occur in life that can make you a more attractive candidate for life insurance than others. People who have recently been married, recently bought a home, or recently had a baby, are now more attractive prospects than others. Market research companies can provide, at a cost, a database of who, in a given geographical area, has encountered any of the aforementioned changes in their life. You still have to make one thousand phone calls, but now there is a rhyme and reason behind your cold calling. You are now cold calling qualified prospects and your chances of success increase dramatically.

Here is something that can help you deal with the mental and physical stress associated with cold calling. The mental stress comes from the rejection, the physical stress comes from the time it takes associated with cold calling, it can be tiring and can wear you out. In baseball you can strike out two hundred times, but hit fifty home runs. What number is more significant, the amount of strike outs or the number of home runs? The number of strike outs is insignificant if you hit home runs. The point is that you need to get in the batter's box. If you are not in the batter's box, you will not have a chance to hit the home run, so who cares how many times you strike out?

The opposite end of the continuum of prospecting are warmer calling techniques such as referrals and networking. Asking satisfied customers if there is anyone else that they can think of that may have a need for your product (referrals) is a prospecting tool that can be effective. Name dropping does work and can help melt the ice associated with cold calling. It can get you over the hurdle of the prospect questioning you how did you get their name or contact information. It can get the conversation started and give you credibility with your new prospect. Networking involves building a database of contacts, who have other contacts, who have additional contacts that all at some day in time can benefit each other. Trade associations and college alumni associations are advantageous sources for networking and often schedule networking events for business professionals to meet other business professionals with the sole purpose of networking. Websites have entered the networking game such as Facebook and LinkedIn and are becoming excellent resources for prospecting. Additional sources of prospecting are trade shows, trade publications, and all kinds of databases that can be found on-line. Some salespeople are good on the phone, some prefer to show up, and some can favor email. Whatever the method, there are several methods of prospecting, and you need to find which one you are comfortable with and incorporate this into your daily sales activity. The point is that you have to prospect, it has to be ingrained in your head, an indelible imprint that needs to be tattooed on your soul as a salesperson.

Approach

Prospecting is a funnel where a ton of names of potential customers are dumped into, filtered, and sanitized and a few make it through the separation process of prospects and suspects. What do you do next? How do you approach the list of customers that the funnel has spit out and dumped in your lap? You will only get one chance to make a first impression on your customer, so you do not want to waste the opportunity. How you approach the customer is vital to the process.

Approach is your initial contact with the customer. Your approach has to be accompanied by an immediate value statement that catches the attention of the customer. Your approach is a prelude to the next step in the process, presentation and demonstration, but you need to get to that step. An effective approach can inaugurate the footing of a successful presentation and demonstration. What does it mean when a customer says, "I will give you a few minutes?" Understand they are busy, they have a job to do, and you need to understand where you fit in their totem pole of importance. You are lucky if you are near the top, most times you are not. You need to respect their time, if you do not, you can ruin the opportunity. When they say I will give you a few minutes, only take a few minutes, it is up to them to send out signals that they will give you more of their valuable time. In your value statement you need to introduce yourself to them, always thank them for taking the time to meet with you, and tell them how you can help them solve their problem. An old axiom was to have an "elevator speech", a brief statement that you would say to a customer if you bumped into them on an elevator that grabs their attention and can lead you to the next step.

Selling is always confrontational, even if you are making a sales call on an existing customer, who can be a friend, they know that when you walk in the door you are attempting to sell them something. You need to break the ice, make them relax, make them feel comfortable and not confrontational. This all falls under the category of developing rapport with a customer. People buy products from people they like, and there is nothing wrong with trying to develop a relationship, or rapport with a customer.

Look for signals when you walk into their office to approach them. You head needs to be on a swivel, and you need to have eyes in the back of your head to see what type of environment you are walking into. Is it a good time, or does it seem like it is not? Again, they are busy and can be having a bad day. If they are having a bad day they might want to spread the misery and ruin your day as well. Understand, most buyers resent commission, or a better way to state it is that they know that you are financially benefiting by them saying, "Yes, I will take it." If they are having a tough day, why should they make your day? Signals can include a busy desk that is filled with work, a phone that does not stop ringing, an assistant that keeps interrupting your meeting, or in today's world a computer that keeps making a noise alerting the customer that they just received an email. You need the mood in the room to be conducive to a positive, selling environment. If it does not look like it is a good time, do not be ashamed to ask the customer if you can reschedule your meeting when it is a better time for them. Their time is valuable, your time is insignificant to them.

During your approach if you ascertain that the environment is right, you then should look for items in their office that say something about their life. Customers spend a tremendous amount of time in their office and will often decorate it to make it feel like they are at home. Customers love to talk about themselves and striking up a conversation about something that you spot in their office can help build rapport with the customer. Family pictures on their desk, a diploma on the wall, a trophy or award that they might have won, or even something that shows their allegiance to a favorite sports team. You have to be careful, if they have a picture of a baby on their desk, and it is not a cute baby, do not say something like, "Oh my gosh, that is the cutest baby I have ever seen." They know the baby is not that cute, because nobody has ever said that and they can see right through your intentions. If you notice that the diploma on the wall is from a rival school that you attended, do not mention it. If their favorite sports team is a bitter rival of yours, do not even go there. If they have pictures of something that is very specific, that they seem to have an interest in, but you only have a casual interest in, skip that one too, because they might be an expert on the topic, and you will lose your credibility and destroy the rapport that you might have built up with the customer. If you share a common interest, or share a common family life cycle occurrence then it can help to build rapport. You need to remember that customers like to talk about THEIR lives, and might not be so interested in yours. So keep your side of the story brief.

Once rapport has been established, and you have preceded to get them to relax, you need to move to the next step in the approach process which is to prepare to get to the next step of presentation and demonstration. At this point the direction of the conversation has to shift their way. Too many salespeople do too much talking. You need to be quiet and let them explain why they have agreed to meet with you. Obviously they have a problem, which translates into a need. Let them state the problem. You are a detective on a crime scene. Gather information that helps you to decipher the problem. You are in the need discovery stage of the approach process. If you determine that the customer has a problem (need) that you can solve with your product being the solution to their problem, then you should gather as much information as possible for you to move to the next step in the sales process which is presentation and demonstration. If you determine that at this time you cannot provide a solution to their problem, thank them for their time and move on to your next prospect. This customer will respect that you did not push a product on them that will not satisfy their needs, and keep you in mind down the road when their needs might change.

Presentation and Demonstration

Preparation is the key to making a successful sales presentation and demonstration. There is no such thing as being too prepared, or overly prepared for a presentation and demonstration. The day that you leave a sample in your car, or piece of literature or brochure behind, is the day that you will need it for your presentation. Always prepare for the worst, because if you are prepared for the worst then you can handle any quirk or curveball that is thrown your way.

Expect the technology that you are using for your presentation to fail, expect your product to malfunction during your presentation, expect to have problems with the room that you are planning for your presentation, and expect your customer to cut you short on the time that they told you will be allotted for your presentation. If you are prepared for this and any other circumstances that can pop up to sabotage your presentation and demonstration you will be fine.

What can happen with the technology that you are using for your presentation? What if your laptop is not compatible with the overhead that the customer provides? What can happen to your product? What if it fails to turn on, or not perform the way it is supposed to? What can happen to the room that you expect to make your presentation in? What if the room is too small, where you do not have enough room to make your presentation, or too large where your presentation is hard to hear? What if the heat is not working during the winter or the air conditioning is not functioning during the summer? What if you were told that you have one hour to make your presentation and demonstration only to find out that when you arrive at your meeting you only have fifteen minutes to get your message across? All of these circumstances can alter the delivery of your presentation and demonstration. The more that you are prepared the better you will be able to handle adjustments that you may need to make in your presentation and demonstration. You need to remain calm, cool, and collected and the best way to depict this behavior is if you are prepared.

Do not just bring your laptop with your presentation on it, bring a thumb drive with a copy of your presentation on it in case you have laptop problems. Email a copy of your presentation to yourself and the customer in case you have to pull up your presentation from an alternative device. Make hard copies of your presentation and bring them with you in case your technology fails, if they say that ten people will be at the meeting make fifteen copies. You never know who will show up for your presentation. What if additional participants show up, including senior members of management of your customer's organization, you want to have copies for everyone. Have multiple samples of your product with you in case of a product malfunction. Show up early to check out the room where you will be making your presentation, so that you will have the opportunity to anticipate any room distractions that you may encounter. Be prepared to shorten your presentation from the time that they have allotted.

There are two elements that are common denominators of most sales presentations, a salesperson and a customer. Salespeople make common presentations to the same kind of customer every day. It behooves a company to make sure that a salesperson is delivering the proper message to the customer. During the sales training process it is crucial to educate your salespeople on what to say when you get in front of a customer. A common method is to develop a script, or memorized presentation, where the salesperson recites the same verbiage, in all of their presentations. Another word for this is a "canned" presentation which is a packaged and manufactured set of words that can assist a salesperson specifically when they are new to a company, product, and industry.

Scripted sales presentations are successful because they are filled with words and phrases that have worked for other seasoned sales people who have been successful. Why not replicate what has worked in the past. Some companies take it too far and force their new salespeople, right out of sales training, to say the exact same thing to every customer that they make a sales presentation to. They want all of their salespeople on the same page, and they want them to duplicate the message that has worked for successful salespeople. A downside of the scripted sales presentation is that the salesperson can sound programmed and rote. The scripted presentation is void of personal inflection. The scripted presentation is by the book, word for word. Yet, the scripted presentation can be effective. The key for sales success is to start with the scripted sales presentation and as you become more comfortable with the delivery of your message to inject your own personality into the scripted presentation. Every day that you become more acclimated with the delivery of your message, you should start to subtract words from the scripted speech. Over a period of time, once you become comfortable with your words and delivery of your message, you will become less dependent on the scripted sales presentation and more dependent on your own words that make your presentation more genuine.

It is imperative to tailor and customize your presentation to your audience. Many of your presentations and demonstrations will have commonalities, but the customization of the presentation and demonstration comes from the information that you obtained during your initial approach meeting. If you give your standard, generic presentation and demonstration that includes elements of your presentation and demonstration that you give to all of your customers, it can include information that does not pertain to the current presentation. Customers can be distracted and lose interest during your presentation because you are discussing product features and benefits that are not relevant to their situation. However, if your presentation and demonstration is tailored to their needs, it can be an indication that you did listen to their concerns during the initial approach meeting and increase your credibility.

Show and tell has been a popular method to make a demonstration that dates all the way back to when you were in kindergarten. The most effective product demonstrations are the most realistic product demonstrations that place a product in the hands of a potential customer so they can see firsthand the features and benefits that the product can offer. If possible, place a sample of your product in the hands of the prospective customer. Let them touch and feel the product, let them sample and evaluate the product. If they try the product, and like the product, they might buy the product. During the demonstration it is paramount for you to validate the ease of use of your product. The more comfortable that they become with your product because of an effective demonstration, the better the chance of closing the sale. It is essential to get the customer involved in the demonstration process. You can verbalize features and benefits to a customer, but it can be convenient for them not to remember a word that you have said. You can exhibit the features and benefits of your product in front of your customer and they will have a better chance of retaining the information. If you solicit the participation of your customer in a "hands on" demonstration of the features and benefits of your product, the probability of the customer retaining an increased comprehension can be maximized.

Body language and room logistics are elements of the presentation and demonstration that often are overlooked. In a one on one meeting, when you walk into the room, after you look around to scan the environment, where is the best place to sit? The worst place to sit, which is often where you will end up, is directly across the desk from the customer. Face-to- face, eye-to-eye, why is this the worst place to sit? It is the worst place, but the most common place to sit, because face-to-face, and eye-to-eye, represents confrontation. If possible sit on the same side of the desk as the customer. Side by side is more of a collaborative approach, we are on the same side of the problem and not as confrontational. Getting a seat behind a customer's desk right next to them is tough, and can be a challenge, people become protective of their space, and entering or invading that space can become problematic. What if they have a separate table in their office, adjacent to their desk, ask them to sit there and when they get up from their desk to sit at the table sit next to them. This also gets them away from the work that is on their desk, their phone, computer, and any notes that are in front of them. If possible get them out of their office element, customers are chained to their desks, and welcome a reason to get to vacate their desk. Take them to a coffee shop, or out for breakfast, lunch, or dinner to get them away from the distraction of their desk. In a committee presentation or demonstration in front of a group of customers, it is important to watch where everyone sits. Never discount any participant's role in the committee, you never know who has the power and influence over the group. Usually there is a leader, or chairperson, who has the most influence. Watch where they sit, most times it is either at the end of the table or in the middle. You need to spot the body language of the group, usually the group will defer to the chairperson, so within a few minutes you need to determine who in the room is running the show, and who is just a spectator.

During your presentation and demonstration you need to gauge how it is going, and a message that is sent to you is the body language that your customer indirectly communicates to you. If a customer is leaning towards you with their arms open, it can be a signal that they are interested and are looking for help to solve their problem. If the customer has their arms crossed, they do not believe a word that you are saying. If they are staring at their watch, looking at their computer screen, checking their phone, or simply looking out the window, they are not listening to a word that you are saying. Who do you have a better chance of moving to the next step with? A customer who just sits there with no response, or a customer who interrupts every word you say with a question or objection to what you are saying? An interruption or question is great. It shows you that they are listening to what you are saying, are interested in what you are saying, you have said something that has struck a chord, spurred their interest, and compelled them to say something.

Customers can ask all kinds of questions during your presentation and demonstration. There are good questions, questions that are on point and questions that can come from left field. You need to be able to think on your feet. Thinking on your feet means that you need to be able to digest the question and give the best response that you can, on the spot. Remember, the more that you repeat your presentation and demonstration, the more comfortable that you will become. You sell the same product every day in front of the same type of customer. The questions are similar. A salesperson makes so many presentations that the salesperson should know what can hook the customer and what can drive a customer away from making the sale.

What do you do when a customer asks you a great, on point question that you cannot answer? Do you change the subject? Do you distract the audience? Do you spin the question around and respond with an answer that does not really answer the question? Understand, the customer does not know that you do not have an answer to their question, to them it is just a question, to you it is a question that you cannot answer. If you distract the audience they might forget about the question. The best way to answer the question that you cannot answer is to acknowledge to the customer that it is a great question, and that you are not sure and you will get back to them. Write the question down in front of them. If possible pick up the phone and call your sales manager or headquarters and try to get an answer to the question on the spot. This will increase your credibility with the customer. If you cannot get an immediate response, get an answer back to the customer as soon as you can. Record that great question in the back of your mind, because it can come up again, as early as tomorrow in your next presentation or demonstration, and now you will prepared to answer the question in front of your next customer.

Proof is the ultimate element of your presentation and demonstration that you can hold in your back pocket that can get you to the next step in the sales process. Popular questions from customers can be, "Why should I buy your product? Who else uses your product?" If you respond with, "A majority of the customers in this market have been long standing customers of mine" and you begin to rattle off a few names of satisfied customers, it can help your cause. If these are top, well respected customers, that reference alone can sway the customer in your direction. An example would be, "What other hospitals are using your product?" If you are able to recite the names of the top hospitals in your territory, or other names of famous hospitals around the country who are using your product, it can help. An attitude that can circulate around the room is that, "If it is good for them, maybe we should consider it too." Of course the opposite can work against you, what if your reference list of customers are not the best hospitals in town? This can hamper your progress and slow down the sales process.

Marketing data can work in your favor as a proof statement as well, Market share data where you are able to spew out data that you are the market leader, or at least give you the opportunity to state your position in the marketplace, or in the case of the pharmaceutical and medical device industry who rely on published clinical studies that can prove the efficacy of their product. The more proof that you have, the easier it is to dispel the doubt that can be going through the mind of your customer.

Handling Objections

Not everyone is going to agree with everything you say in every sales presentation that you make. If every customer said, "I'll take it!" everyone would become a salesperson. There is a humungous misconception about a customer making an objection during your sales presentation and a customer rejecting your sales presentation. Objection is not rejection and there needs to be clarification of the two. Rejection means no. Rejection means I am not interested. Rejection means this meeting is over. Rejection means, "Do not call me, I will call you!" Objections are good. Objections should be welcomed. Objections are a request for more information. Objections show interest in your sales presentation. Objections mean that the customer is interested in something that you have said in your presentation and demonstration, but they have a question that you need to clarify. Common objections include price, quality, delivery date, competitive offerings, product features, and product functionality. A shrewd technique to overcome a product objection is to encourage that the customer participates in the demonstration process.

Price is the most frequent objection that you will hear. "That's so expensive? Why do you charge so much? I cannot afford that? I do not have the dollars in my budget!" You should never be ashamed about the price that you charge. You might have to defend that price, and justify that price, but you should never be ashamed to charge that price. You need to make a value statement that validates your price. Value statements can reflect the quality of your components, the research and development, or software and technology that goes into the manufacturing process and is reflected by the price you charge. Value-added items that are included in your proposal must be highlighted, because they are items that you do not typical charge for, but are thrown in as part of the deal. There is a cost associated with value-added items that does not get passed on to the customer. Popular value-added items can include free samples, training, or extended warrantees. The more value-added items that can be included in your proposal, or added to your proposal when the objection of price is raised, the better the chance of overcoming the objection.

You need to be optimistic when overcoming the objection of price. There are softer words and techniques that you can use to ease the pain associated with the price that you are going to charge. You want to avoid, "sticker shock", where the customer looks at your proposal and is immediately turned off by the price that you are proposing. The words that you choose to use can help get over the hurdle. Which sounds better, "This costs $495, or this is only $495?" Replacing the word cost with the word only is a more subtle, softer message. What about this example, "Your down payment will be ten percent, or your initial investment will be ten percent." Switching out the word down payment with the words initial investment can be more effective.

The more presentations that you make, the more experienced that you become at anticipating where the meeting is going. You need to be able to take the temperature of the situation, to gauge the level of interest of the customer. You make the same presentation every day in front the same type of customer. You know who is really interested and who is not. You say a lot of the same things every day, and so does the customer. If you get to the point of your presentation where objections are usually raised, it is wise to forestall the objection. Forestalling the objection means that you address the objection before the customer makes the objection. You can sense that the objection is coming, so you are better off addressing the objection before the customer makes the objection. Other tips are to handle the objections as they occur. You do not want the objections to pile up and then you are spending too much time responding to the multiple objections that are preventing you to go to the next step, closing the sale. You should always let the customer state the objection, hear them out, and do not interrupt their concerns. If it is a legitimate objection, acknowledge the objection, comprehend the objection, confirm that it is a great question they have raised and respond accordingly.

Some objections are concealed and problematic to respond to because the customer is not as forthcoming as you would like them to be. They might not be ready to make a decision, the need for your product can be disguised, or they simply need more time to evaluate, or think about their alternatives. Pushy salespeople respond to this objection, by stating that they have answered all of your questions, and push to move to the close. Problem solving salespeople understand that it takes time to make the decision to purchase a product, answer the objections the best that they can, and let the customer breathe a little bit, to give them the opportunity to make the decision on their terms, when they are ready. If you have satisfied all of the customer's concerns (objections), and you have leaped over this giant hurdle, you are now staring at the most important step in the selling process, closing the sale.

Closing the Sale

Most salespeople can be trained to get to this step. You can be trained on how to get better at prospecting, better at approaching the customer, better at presenting and demonstrating your product, and better at handling objections. Closing the sale is what separates the average salesperson from the good salesperson. It delineates the great salesperson from the good salesperson, and it becomes a line of demarcation between the great salesperson and the super-star salesperson. Hands down, closing the sale is the most significant step in the sales process. It is the most arduous step in the process, because the close is where you are asking for a commitment from the customer. You are reaching in their pocket and taking their money. Customers like their money, and are not as enthusiastic about parting with their money as you would like them to be. Without the close there is no bullion, there is no treasure, there is no gold.

From the first time that a company puts out a job advertisement or job posting, in the job description is states, "Must have a documented history of closing sales, or strong closing skills required, only top closers apply." The job description never says, "Looking for prospecting experts, or experienced sales demonstration skill required." The same goes for the interview process. Yes, it is a good idea during an interview to mention that you love to prospect, and that cold calling is something that you truly enjoy, and you will be asked to explain your interpretation of the sales process, but the sales manager will specifically ask you to describe the biggest, hardest, or most challenging sales close that you have had in your career. All of the other steps can be taught or enhanced through sales training and sales development, but closing skills are tough to teach. Closing skills are not only tough to teach, but they are tough to learn, and closing skills are tough to master. There is an innate characteristic that must be brought out in a salesperson that can make them better at closing sales.

Do you need to follow all of the steps in the sales process, in the actual order that has been depicted? The answer is no. There is an old rule of thumb, ABC, ALWAYS BE CLOSING. You should be closing the sale from the minute that you introduce yourself to the customer.

The customer might be ready sooner than you think, and you do not want to talk yourself out of making a sale. You should use a trial close technique. A trial close means that you are "trying" to close the sale as you go through your presentation and demonstration. A trial close is a stab, during your presentation or demonstration, to inspire the customer to take the necessary action and make the purchase of your product.

Negotiation needs to change as salespeople move away from the transaction selling model towards the more professional relationship selling model. In the transaction model negotiation is a win-lose mentality. The salesperson wins and the customer loses. The salesperson tries to sell their product at the highest price possible. Salespeople can be persuasive, convincing, and charming. The more skilled that they are at this, the higher the price they can negotiate for their product. They start the negotiation high and only come down on their price when they feel the sale is slipping through their fingers.

Everybody loves making a deal, getting a good deal on a product. Transaction salespeople love the back and forth banter and haggling between the salesperson and the customer. Let's say that the salesperson starts the negotiation at ten and the customer counters with five, the salesperson comes down to nine, the customer goes up to six, the salesperson come down to eight, the salesperson goes up to seven, the salesperson comes down to seven and they make a deal. Yes, the higher the price that you can negotiate, the higher the commission that you make. This can also include an escalating commission structure, that not only will you make more commission on the sale, the percentage of commission can increase the higher the price that you negotiate.

Here is the problem with this negotiation. If I am the customer I look at you and say, "Hey, you tried to sell me this item at ten, and the only reason why you came down to seven is because I complained that the price was too high." In the customer's eyes, the salesperson tried to take advantage of them and the situation. This does not help forge a long-term relationship between the salesperson and the customer, and fosters resentment that can force the customer to look elsewhere the next time they are in the market for the product.

Negotiation is a painful experience. It is your job to minimize the amount of pain at the negotiating table. No is a bad word during negotiation. You do not want the word no in the room. In the relationship selling model negotiation needs to be a win-win situation, where both sides give in a little, but both sides have a good feeling about the negotiation, and at the end of the day both sides win. What defines a win-win situation? A fair deal defines a win-win situation. What's a fair deal? A fair deal is a price that is comparable to what other customers have paid for the same product. A fair deal is what your competitors are charging for a comparable product. The market should dictate the price, not the salesperson. The salesperson needs to sell value, not only the value of your product, but the value that you bring to the table as a sales professional, and the value your company brings to the table.

In the above example if seven is a fair price, that the market has established, then the salesperson should walk in to the negotiation with the price of seven on their mind. A half a loaf of bread is better than no bread at all. No one is saying to walk into a negotiation and drop the drawers of your price immediately, or give a product away just to make a sale. You are entitled to make a living. Stand your ground, seven is a fair price, but don't budge off of seven. Some salespeople feel you need to start high and come down, leave yourself some wiggle room. It is a legitimate argument but the point is not to start too high, because you can lose credibility, and the word no begins to creep into the conversation.

Negotiation has been neutralized and in essence salespeople have been neutered. There was a time when buyers did not have as much choice as they have today. Their choices were limited to the expensive alternative and the cheapest alternative. Today there is too much choice, there might not be an exact match for an alternative product, but it can be close enough that if the buyer is not happy with the negotiation, they can take their business elsewhere. Buyers are smarter today. Understand, a purchasing agent for a company spends the entire day purchasing products and negotiates with salespeople all day, every day. Just as you are a professional salesperson who sells products all day, they are professional buyers, and professional shoppers, who can be experts at their craft as well. Buyers listen to sales pitches all day, they have heard every kind of sales pitch imaginable, they have seen every closing tactic and closing technique, and can see right through a proposal that is not a win-win situation. Professional buyers attend conferences and seminars that teach them how to spot unethical behavior among salespeople. They learn how to play one vendor against another, and are taught how to squeeze out every nickel during a negotiation. There is software and there are websites that list competitive prices that buyers can access, so the days of sweet talking your way towards a sale or pulling the wool over the eyes of the customer are over.

As noted earlier, the time that you spend during the sale process to get the customer to this point can be monumental. At this point you have still not made the sale, and all of your efforts still can go down the tubes overnight. If you have invested all of this time, remember, the quota clock has been ticking during all of the steps of the sales process, and you have not had any return on the investment of your time. There becomes a time during the close to get a little heavy handed and ask the customer for the order. Are they going to move forward or not?

You need to know where you stand. There is a professional way to take this approach and also a pushy way to take this approach. If you ask an open ended question, which gives the customer the chance to elaborate and verbalize exactly where you stand in the sales process, it gives them the opportunity to voice any concerns or objections that they may still have. An example of an open ended question can be, "Are there any questions that you may have, or any details that we have not discussed that you need to have clarified before we move further?" The open ended question is soliciting a lengthy response filled with words. If you can satisfy their concerns then you can start to ask closed ended questions. Closed ended questions solicit short, one or two word responses, usually, yes or no responses. Examples of closed ended questions are, "Have we identified that you have a need for my product? Are you the sole decision maker who is making the decision to purchase this product?" The closed ended question is used as a confirmation and clarification tool.

The pushy salesperson utilizes high pressure closing tactics such as, "If you do not take advantage of this deal today, I am not sure if I can guarantee this price tomorrow, or if you do not buy this product today, I have other customers lined up who are ready and I cannot guarantee that this product will be there when you are ready to buy?"

Preparation is a consistent thread that is sprinkled throughout the steps in the sales process. Asking for the order becomes more routine if the salesperson is tactically prepared for the close. Salespeople become gun shy when they get to the close. Not asking for the order is a huge mistake, or just asking for the order only once can also be a mistake. Do not be bashful or gun shy, to get to this point in the process you have already established a relationship with this customer, and have developed a rapport with this customer, and now is the time to cash in, cross the finish line, complete the task at hand, CLOSE the sale!

You need to exude self-confidence during the close. You need to be relaxed during the close, and you need the customer to relax during the close. If you are self-confident and relaxed, this can permeate and come across to the customer that they are making the right decision. If you are rushed, unprepared, and nervous, it can come across that you are not so sure that this is a great proposal that you have put on the table. If you are prepared for the close you can minimize and avoid any surprises at the close. Surprises can include last minute requests by the customer, eleventh hour last minute proposal changes, and desperate competitive bids that can be a scare tactic. You need to be poised and professional, you need to believe in your product, and that your product is the solution to the customer's problem. This sincerity will be transmitted to the customer and they can look at you as a true problem solver.

Follow-Up

In the transaction model of selling, closing the sale was the final step in the sales process. Once you close the sale, you have made your commission and the next step is to start the process all over again and begin to prospect for your next customer. That has been changed today, where the importance of post-sale follow-up and service has become a critical element of the sales process.

Salespeople are like politicians, or is it the other way around, politicians are like salespeople? When politicians are running for political office, they are filled with promises. "If you vote for me I promise to do this, and I promise to do that." Election day is comparable to the close in the sales process. Did you win the election, did you close the sale? Follow-up is the time after the election when the politician needs to come through on their campaign promises that got them elected. If they do not come through on their promises they will not be re-elected. It is the same thing in sales. Salespeople make statements (promises), and for the record, never promise a customer something that you cannot deliver on, during the aforementioned steps in the sales process. "If you buy my product it can do this for you, If you buy my product my company can do that for you, if you buy my product I will do this for you." Follow-up presents the forum to come through on your insinuations. If you want to get re-elected you will need to be true to your promises, if you want to have a long-term relationship with your customers you need to follow-up.

What infuriates customers about salespeople? Is it the pushy, aggressive approach, the never ending hounding? All of the above. What annoys a customer the most is a salesperson who seems to be pushing and annoying them to make a purchase, then once the purchase is made, the salesperson cannot be found. The salesperson cannot be found because they are following the transaction model where they made their commission and have moved on to their next victim (customer). It gives the customer the impression that they have been duped, they have been had, and they proceed to place the salesperson on top of the pile of salespeople who run after they make the sale. Following-up with the customer means that you will be there, you will be available, you will be around after the sale is made. A successful follow-up technique is to contact the customer within a few days of making the sale. Contact them to thank them for the business, contact them to ask them if they have any questions, any concerns, and let them know that you are around to ease them into the implementation of your product. The tip is to call them before they call you. If you intercept their call before hand, it will show the customer that you have not run away, and that you are available and you are there to help them with the transition to your product.

You can find out what day you product will be delivered to your customer, so show up that day. There can be all kinds of problems associated with the delivery of your product, did they get the correct items, in the correct quantities? You might have to unpack the boxes to ascertain and confirm that the order received is exactly what they ordered. If the boxes sit on their loading dock, how do you know that the customer is satisfied? If your product requires assembly or installation, be there to assist in the process. Product implementation can be a process. A successful implementation makes for a successful long-term relationship. An unsuccessful implementation opens the door for blame. Customers never blame themselves, the finger is always pointed at the salesperson who pushed them into making the decision to purchase the product. Reduce the chance of blame, become the point person in the implementation process. Be there on the day that the customer goes live with you product, the first day that they are actually using your product, it can minimize the stress associated with the utilization of a new product. Training the customer on how to use your product is crucial to the implementation. If they are not trained properly, they will not use the product in the desired manner. If they do not use the product correctly, because they were not trained properly, it can open the door for complaints and doubts. Salespeople do not want to open that door.

An example of follow-up with a customer that can lead to a win-win situation is the way that product returns are handled. For the most part when a purchase is made, a sale is a sale, and once the customer has taken delivery of a product it is theirs. Initial mistakes with orders aside, are a different story and most good companies will allow a grace period of time to send back or exchange products that have been ordered. What happens when that grace period has expired? What if an expiration date has been passed, what if the style and model of a product has been upgraded, what if the packaging on your product has changed? What do you do with this excess inventory that is not selling, and your customer is not happy because of the perception that they are stuck with it? This can hamper or impede the long-term relationship that you are trying to establish with your customer. You want the customer to place additional orders for your product, but they cannot because they are loaded up with product that they cannot sell. It can be an odd size, or uncommon color, whatever the issue it needs to be resolved.

You as the salesperson can facilitate a solution where everyone wins. You are in the middle between your company and your customer. If you approach your customer with a proposal that you will exchange out all of the unwanted inventory, but they need to replace it with new items that will sell, plus add an additional amount to their purchase. An example would be that if they had one thousand dollars of old inventory, and they placed an order for thirteen hundred dollars of new sellable inventory. They get rid of the old stock, and you make an additional thirty percent on the new merchandise. The company accepts the return and can repackage the items, donate the product, or write it off as an expense. Why would the company do this, the product that has been replaced can spur sales for the customer because it is new inventory and can lead to additional repeat business when this batch of inventory is sold. The customer benefits because they shed themselves of the unwanted inventory, and the salesperson wins because they make an additional sale and receive the residual benefits of future sales of the fresh inventory. A win for everyone! This is the type of follow-up and service that creates a bond between the salesperson and customer that once established is hard to compete against.

Post-purchase behavior, or how a customer reacts after making a purchase is a major element of the follow-up process. Cognitive dissonance, or how a customer feels after making a purchase is something that needs to be measured. Cognitive means thinking, and dissonance refers to a bad feeling. How do your customers feel after making a purchase? Do they doubt the decision, or are they thrilled with the decision to purchase your product? Salespeople need to reduce the level of cognitive dissonance and the way to do this is to walk the customer through the entire follow-up process.

Does this mean that you have to morph into more of a service technician than a salesperson, the answer is yes. Salespeople have a problem with this metamorphosis because you are not being paid to be a service technician, you are being paid to sell. This irritates salespeople because the quota clock is ticking and if you are spending too much time following-up it can distract you from starting the sales process again with a new customer. All of these follow-up techniques are designed with one goal in mind, a long-term relationship with your customer. Once you complete the process with one customer you need to start the process again with your next customer. If you build a territory populated with satisfied customers they will call you back again when they are in the market for another product. If you followed up on your promises that you made during the earlier steps in the sales process, you can bypass most of the previous steps and shorten the sales cycle. Your prospecting time is cut down, presentation and demonstration is in the rear view mirror, and closing and negotiation is not as painful the second time around. It is all about time management, the quota clock is still ticking, and you can shave off valuable time in the process if you have a satisfied customer.

Chapter 11

....

Motivation of the Salesperson: Why Get Out of Bed Every Day?

Motivation is a force that energizes, directs, and sustains behavior. Motivation is behaviorally specific, that is, it is more appropriate to think in terms of a salesperson's motivation to excel in a particular job requirement, or even carry out a specific behavior, than it is to think about a salesperson's overall motivation. While individual dispositional variables may affect a salesperson's motivation level at any particular time, motivation itself is not a disposable variable.

Vroom's Expectancy Theory

Vroom's Expectancy Theory has been selected as one of the theoretical foundations of this book. It is a cognitive theory from organizational behavior that has attracted considerable attention in the sales force management literature. Expectancy theory has become a dominant paradigm for research on motivation in the workplace, and has generated a number of empirical studies[120]. Expectancy theory suggests that motivation depends on the expectations of individuals about their ability to perform tasks and receive desired rewards. Expectancy theory is not concerned with identifying types of needs, but with the thinking process that individuals use to determine the level of motivation for a specific task.

Performance expectancy involves whether putting effort into a task will lead to high performance. For this expectancy to be high, variables such as sales ability, sales experience, sales tools, and the opportunity to perform must be present. Products that require technical expertise, or compete in an aggressive, cut-throat marketplace, need a seasoned or talented salesperson to persuade the customer to buy their product. Sales tools and promotional support range from product advertisement, product samples, product literature and any other support mechanism that can help sell a product. In this age of information technology sales tools have taken on a new meaning. Salespeople can now be provided with electronic sales tools from email, smart phones, wireless laptops, and tablets with Internet access loaded with presentation software that can dress up a sales presentation in front of a customer. This technology is expensive and requires a significant commitment and investment from an organization. Therefore, if a salesperson possesses the aforementioned variables can they expect to perform and be successful as a salesperson? Are expectancy estimates related to sales ability, sales experience, the amount of sales tools, and promotional support provided by the organization?

Successful organizations, with winning products, integrate models that are blended into the daily sales activity of their salespeople to insure some consistency with regards to sales performance. Outcome expectancy involves whether successful performance will lead to the desired outcome. If a salesperson follows a model of success put in place by the organization, with regards to sales activity in the field, can a salesperson expect to succeed?

Vroom's expectancy theory states that an individual tends to act in a certain way based on the expectation that the act will be followed by a given outcome and on the attractiveness of that outcome to the individual. Vroom described expectancy as a subjective probability of an action of effort leading to an outcome or performance[121]. Expectancy theory can be utilized to help understand how salespeople make decisions regarding various behavioral alternatives. The expectancy model deals with the direction aspect of motivation, that is, once behavior is energized, what behavioral alternatives are salespeople likely to pursue? The process of motivation in relation to compensation can be described by three independent variables: effort-performance expectancy, performance-outcome expectancy, and valence.

Vroom's theory included these three variables or relationships:

1) Expectancy (Effort-Performance Linkage) is the probability perceived by the individual that exerting a given amount of effort will lead to a certain level of performance.
2) Instrumentality (Performance-Reward Linkage) is the degree to which the individual believes that performing at a particular level is instrumental in leading to the attainment of a desired outcome.
3) Valence (Attractiveness of Reward) is the importance that the individual places on the potential outcome or reward that can be achieved on the job. Valence considers both the goals and the needs of the individual.

Vroom defined the concept of valence as all possible affective orientations towards outcomes, and it is interpreted as the importance, attractiveness, desirability, or anticipated satisfaction with outcomes. The valence of outcome model states that the valence, or satisfaction, of an outcome is a monotonically increasing function of the algebraic sum of the products of the valences of all other outcomes[122].

Variables affecting a salesperson's valence for outcomes include values, needs, goals, and preferences. Specific demographic characteristics of individual salespeople such as marital status, number of dependents, and standard of living can alter a salesperson's needs and goals. These variables rely more on the individual salesperson's sources of motivation. Outcomes desired by an individual are considered positively valent and those they wish to avoid negatively valent; therefore valences are scaled over a virtually unbounded range of positive and negative values[123].

Vroom characterized the idea of instrumentality as an outcome-outcome association, and it has been interpreted not only as a relationship between an outcome and another outcome, but also as a probability to obtain an outcome[124]. Variables that can affect a salesperson's instrumentality perception are trust, control, and policies. When salespeople trust their sales managers, they are more apt to have confidence that their promises about exceeding sales quota objectives will be rewarded. When salespeople do not trust their sales managers, they often attempt to control the reward system through some type of control mechanism. When salespeople believe that they have some kind of control over how, when, and why rewards are distributed, instrumentality can increase. The degree to which compensation programs are formalized in written policies can have an impact on a salesperson's instrumentality perceptions. Formalized policies connecting rewards to performance tend to increase instrumentality.

The central theme of expectancy theory, is the rather simple concept that an individual's behavior is a function of the degree to which the behavior is instrumental in the attainment of some outcomes, and evaluation of these outcomes[125]. Historically, this conception of motivation had its origins in the Ancient Greek principle of hedonism, which assumes that behavior is directed toward pleasure and away from pain. The individual will choose from alternative courses of action that behavior which they think will maximize their pleasure and minimize their pain [126]. Vroom suggested that people consciously choose particular courses of action, based upon perception, attitudes, and beliefs, as a consequence of their desires to enhance pleasure and avoid pain[127].

Expectancy theory is commonly defined as a belief concerning the likelihood (probability) that focusing a given amount of effort on a particular task will result in an increased level of performance on that task. Expectancy theory clearly communicates the linkages between job effort and performance; and performance and rewards. The use of expectancy theory to understand sales force motivation has produced a considerable amount of research[128].

In broad terms, the focal hypothesis of expectancy theory is that, individuals choose between available alternatives in light of their evaluations of the anticipated future consequences of each alternative. Work motivation, treated as a choice between either alternative levels of work performance, is asserted to be one such domain[129].

The prevailing framework for researching salesperson motivation is expectancy theory[130]. Expectancy theory has guided numerous sales management research studies examining the impact of individual (or personal), task, organizational, and environmental variables on expectancies, instrumentalities, and valences[131]. Expectancy theory rests upon a set of assumptions about the decision processes individuals routinely engage in as they establish levels of work effort[132]. The expectancy framework specifies perceptual relationships between an individual's effort, performance, and rewards through three specific components. The first of these components is expectancy of performance. Expectancies are an individual's estimates of the probability that the effort will influence performance. The second component, instrumentality, is also a probability estimate. Instrumentalities are measures of how strongly an individual believes that performance and rewards are linked. The third component of expectancy theory is valence for rewards. Valences are measures of an individual's evaluation of reward desirability[133].

Vroom's expectancy theory has held a major position in the study of work motivation[134]. Vroom's Valence-Instrumentality-Expectancy (VIE Model)[135], in particular, has been the subject of numerous empirical studies[136]. Researchers[137] studied the impact of job commitment, effort, and performance on valences for rewards, while others[138] have investigated the relationship between supervisory style and salesperson expectancies and instrumentalities. Additional studies[139] examined the relationship between performance and expectancy judgments, while others[140] intended to link expectancy theory and leadership concepts to demonstrate that leader interactions with followers permit the establishment of highly motivated working environments.

Understanding what motivates members of the sales force, and how one might control those motivating factors, is an essential aspect of sales force management. A model of the motivation and performance of industrial salespeople was developed.[141] The motivation component of the model was based on the expectancy theory of motivation developed by Vroom[142].

Researchers[143] hypothesized the magnitude of the salesperson's expectancy estimates is related positively to the salesperson's self-esteem, self-perceived ability, and job tenure, and is related negatively to the salesperson's perceived environmental constraints. Findings suggest important aspects of this environment are economic conditions, strength of competition, sales territory potential, and restrictions of product availability. The magnitude of the salesperson's instrumentality estimates was hypothesized to be a function of the degree to which the salesperson feels they have internal control over the events in their life, and their intellectual ability.

Data suggests the growing use of bonus payments in sales force compensation plans to improve sales productivity and to achieve a variety of organizational objectives[144]. A survey of two hundred and sixty-six sales managers and one hundred and ninety-five salespeople was administered. The purpose of the study was to determine if bonus payments help attain selected firm objectives and their usefulness in generating greater salesperson performance[145].

The findings revealed that bonuses may be effective in inducing higher sales productivity because of their flexibility in tying rewards to performance. A major finding from the study revealed that a significant majority of bonus paying companies rely on sales relative to quota as the primary criteria in determining the amount of the bonus award. Expectancy theory supports this concept where performance contingent bonus awards can lead salespeople to anticipate that hard work today will be rewarded later. Findings revealed that bonus payments may be effective in directing salespeople's efforts toward specific organizational objectives.

Prior research had suggested that a salesperson's expectancy estimate, the belief that devoting a certain amount of energy on a specific undertaking, will result in an increased level of achievement on that task, was positively related to their motivation level. The conclusion was that expectancy estimates were an essential component of sales force motivation.

A survey was given to a national sales force of one hundred and fifty-four salespeople. The purpose of the study was to examine the relationships among salesperson performance outcomes, and expectancy estimates. The survey findings suggest that performance attributions have a direct relationship with salesperson expectancy estimates[146]. Performance attribution refers to who, or what, a salesperson ascribes to as being a major factor in their success as a salesperson. The link between performance attribution and expectancy estimates is clear. Salespeople are creatures of habit. If a salesperson reverts to previous successful selling techniques can they expect to be successful? The research findings suggest that organizational support attributions following high self-ratings of performance can result in a positive impact on sales force motivation. The findings also suggest the same processes can have a negative effect on sales force motivation following low self-ratings of performance[147].

Additional results suggest that perceptions of a recent performance level on a task are positively related to the salesperson's expectancy estimate for the task[148]. This study provided valuable insight to the issues surrounding sales force motivation. The study developed a theoretical model linking performance attributions and expectancies. Research on expectancy theory is vital to understanding the antecedents of the expectancy estimates of salespeople, a major component of their motivation. This research extends the expectancy theory literature by explicitly modeling the causal inference process used by salespeople. Meaningful advances in sales force motivation require a process oriented understanding of salesperson attributions[149].

Self-efficacy, goal difficulty, and the perceived control over performance are variables that can affect a salesperson's expectancy perception. These factors affect expectancies by acting as interaction effects. These factors are the cause, while increased or decreased expectancy estimates are the effect. Self-efficacy is a salesperson's belief about their ability to perform a specific behavior effectively. Can the salesperson have faith in the notion that they have the requisite proficiency to execute the expected objectives? Goal difficulty results when sales goals are set too high, or when sales performance expectations are too arduous. This can lead to depleted expectancy perceptions. When salespeople sense that their quota, or objectives, are beyond their capability to realize, their motivation can be decreased as a result of a dwindling expectancy. For expectancy to be elevated, it is essential that salespeople trust that they have some degree of control over the expected outcome. When salespeople comprehend that the outcome is beyond their faculty to persuade, expectancy, and thus motivation is diminished.

If an organization provides the necessary sales tools, promotional support, and sales training, coupled with their ability, and experience of a salesperson, can this raise the expectancy of success by the salesperson? Heightened success by salespeople can lead to an increased level of motivation. This ground work, or foundation, can result in higher expectancies of motivation among salespeople. Motivated salespeople are more efficient, and more effective, and help to create a win-win situation that can lead to improved relations between salespeople and sales management.

Effort-Performance Expectancy Scale

Is there a correlation between the motivation of salespeople, and the expectancy of being successful as a salesperson? The Effort-Performance Expectancy Scale can be used as an instrument to measure a salesperson's perception of their expectancy estimates.

The Effort-Performance Expectancy Scale is an adaptation of House and Dessler's instrument[150]. For each statement below, you are asked to rate how true the statement is as it pertains to your sales job. The scale begins with generic questions related to the level of job satisfaction of the respondent. The scale then poses questions that are specific to the job description of salespeople. The scale concludes with questions that ask pointed questions related to the expectancy of success of salespeople. A score above twenty-seven can indicate that a sales job is in alignment with the foundations associated with expectancy theory. A score below twenty-seven can be a signal that a sales job is deficient when it comes to the principles correlated with expectancy theory. Measuring the effort-performance expectancy variable will grant input into whether the expectancy variable mediates the relationship between the motivation of the salesperson and their expectancy of success.

Exhibit #3: Effort-Performance Expectancy Scale

(Definitely **NOT TRUE** of my job)　　　1　2　3　4　5　　　(Extremely **TRUE** of my job)

1. If I work hard at my job it is likely that I will
   meet high standards of excellence. ＿＿＿

2. Doing things as well as I am capable results
   in completing my assignments on time. ＿＿＿

3. The amount of effort that I place into trying to
   sell my product can directly affect my performance. ＿＿＿

4. If I complete the necessary steps in the sales cycle,
   can I expect the customer to say yes, and purchase
   my product? ＿＿＿

5. If a sale is made can I expect that my company
   and product will live up to expectations made during
   the sales process? ＿＿＿

6. If I am confident in my ability to succeed as a
   salesperson can I expect to be successful? ＿＿＿

7. Does my experience as a salesperson have an influence
   on my expectancy to succeed as a salesperson? ＿＿＿

8. If my company provides me with the necessary sales
   and promotional tools can I expect to be successful? ＿＿＿

9. If I follow a model of success put in place by my company
   that has made previous salespeople successful, can I expect
   to be successful? ＿＿＿

Herzberg's Hygiene-Motivation Theory

Content theories of motivation attempt to explain the factors that motivate individuals through identifying and satisfying their individual needs and desires. A content theory of motivation that can be utilized to better understand how salespeople are motivated is Herzberg's Hygiene-Motivation Theory. Herzberg's theory of motivation postulates that the job environment can be separated into two dimensions: hygiene factors and motivation factors[151]. It is based on the deceptively straightforward idea that motivation can be dichotomized into hygiene factors and motivation factors and is often referred to as a two need system.

Hygiene factors are those that, if insufficient, can cause dissatisfaction on the job. Compensation is a hygiene factor. Can evolving compensation structures affect the daily focus of field selling activity? Can a salesperson maximize the commission opportunity, knowing the commission structure is going to change in the future? How do you motivate salespeople to sell on a daily basis when the salesperson knows that eventually the commission on this transaction is going to change? What role does an incentive compensation plan have on the motivation of salespeople? Other examples of hygiene factors are company policies, working conditions, and relationships with co-workers and supervisors. A sales manager may alleviate dissatisfaction by improving a hygiene factor, but the effects are thought to be temporary and lacking in lasting motivational benefit. Motivation factors in Herzberg's theory include achievement, recognition, challenging work, and the opportunity for growth and advancement. These factors correspond to long-term motivation, job satisfaction, and performance. Can achievement and recognition among a sales force be a motivating factor for a salesperson?

Herzberg's research proved that employees will strive to achieve hygiene needs because they are unhappy without them, but once satisfied the effect soon wears off, satisfaction is temporary. Herzberg's theory concluded that not all job factors can motivate employees. The hygiene factors simply serve to reduce dissatisfaction, whereas it is the motivation factors that produce job satisfaction[152]. A lack of motivators leads to over concentration on hygiene factors, which are those negative factors which can be seen and therefore form the basis of complaint and concern. Hygiene factors lead to dissatisfaction with a job because of the need to avoid unpleasantness. They are referred to as hygiene factors because they can be avoided or prevented by the use of hygienic methods. Herzberg was the first to show that satisfaction and dissatisfaction at work nearly always arose from different factors, and were not simply opposing reactions to the same factors, as had always previously been accepted.

The heart of Herzberg's theory of motivation is that the core motivating factors are not in the environment, but in the intrinsic value and satisfaction gained from the job itself. It follows therefore that to motivate an individual, a job itself must be challenging, have scope for enrichment, and be of interest to the employee. Motivators are those factors directly concerned with the satisfaction gained from a job. Understanding Herzberg's theory recognizes the intrinsic satisfaction that can be obtained from the work itself. It draws attention to job design and makes managers aware that problems of motivation may not necessarily be directly associated with the work. Problems can often be external to the job. Herzberg's theory of motivation has implications related to sales force motivation and sales force management. Salespeople ought to do their best to avoid dissatisfiers. For example, while an insufficient sales training manual, or an industry reputation of customer service deficiencies, will not help sell the company's products, they can easily act as a deterrent in moving a customer towards closing a sale.

Companies need to identify the foremost satisfiers and motivators, features and benefits that describe why customers buy products. These motivators and satisfiers must be articulated and disseminated to the sales force and integrated into daily sales force activity. Motivating and controlling salespeople's activity through quota plans is a widespread industry practice[153]. Traditional sales management literature cites incentives as a catalyst to bring together the goals of salespeople, with the company's goals, and to motivate salespeople to behave in the interest of the company[154].

The reason behind this is clear: Quotas are established to provide salespeople with incentive based goals and objectives that are rewarding and are worth being achieved. The lack of direct supervision makes controlling and motivating field sales people different. Field salespeople operate independently of corporate structures. Controlling and motivating field salespeople can become a challenge to the organization. Compensation plans are used to supervise (control) salespeople and compensation is an important motivator[155].

Dissatisfaction with compensation could be eliminated with a pay raise, but this might not motivate better performance or assure satisfaction beyond the short term. To gain some idea of the challenge associated with providing sufficient hygiene factors, a study on industrial salespeople's views on motivation revealed that eighty percent of salespeople are dissatisfied with their company's compensation policies[156]. Another study was conducted to determine if salespeople's compensation was capped by the organization. Findings revealed that sixty-five percent of the salespeople surveyed said that their compensation earnings were limited by their organization's compensation plan[157].

Motivational Conclusions

You have selected a career in sales, or maybe you are considering a career in sales, or possibly wondering if this is the right career choice. Hopefully this book has helped you to either justify your career decision or at least opened your eyes to provide you with a realistic look at the life of a salesperson. It is a great life, but as with anything in life it comes with challenges that you will need to face. There are so many things in life that are beyond your control, and while there are many things in the life of a salesperson that are still out of your control, this life provides you with the most control of your own destiny.

"There Ain't no Can't." This is a quote from a Trainer/Coach from a famous movie about boxing when the trainer was preparing the boxer for a fight with one of his opponents. It is as grammatically incorrect as a sentence can be, but it is so true. You can do anything that you want in this country, and become anything that you want in this country, but you have to have the desire, work ethic, and perseverance to fight through the obstacles to climb the mountain of success. People will laugh at you, and your lofty aspirations. Expect this, expect people to tell you that you can't do this, and you can't do that. This not only comes from people in your professional life, but people in your personal life, including loved ones. They want to let you down easy.

You know what I say to that? The heck with them, all of them! You have to dig deep down into your inner soul and if you truly have the conviction to complete a task, you would be amazed at what you can accomplish if you put your mind to it.

My entire life I have been told that you can't do this and you can't do that. You can't become this and you can't become that. I have used the word "can't" as a motivational tool and who is left standing? Who has climbed the mountain, who gets the last laugh when you accomplish something, and shut everyone up by saying I can do that and I did do that. It will enhance the thrill of victory.

I was in my last semester of college and I had to make a decision about a job after graduation. Nothing really grabbed my attention. Then one day on the way home I drove past a sporting goods store that was in my neighborhood for decades. There was a For Sale sign in the window. I went home and I thought about it. It sounded like a natural fit, a sports fan, from a sports family, in the sports business. I spoke with my parents about it, and at the age of twenty-one I bought the store. Of course I had to hear it from the detractors, you CAN'T run a business. You know nothing about running a business. What do you know about the business of sports? All legitimate concerns, but again I had to deal with the word "CAN'T". It certainly was not easy and it was one of the steepest mountains that I ever had to climb in my life. I persevered, fought through the growing pains, and turned it into a success. There Ain't no CAN'T.

One day the light when off in my head that I wanted to pursue a career as a professor. I had no formal teacher training, and no teaching experience, yet I still made up my mind that I wanted to pursue this dream. Again, I was saddled with, "You CAN'T become a professor, you don't have an education background, you have no credentials." I needed credentials. The first step was to go back to graduate school. I walked into the dean's office of the university that I graduated from to inquire about attending graduate school. It was the same dean who was there when I was an undergraduate student. In my third year of college she put me on academic probation, which forced me to get my act together, which I did, and I ended up graduating on time a year and a half later. I do owe her a debt of gratitude for straightening me out, setting me straight, and giving me some tough love that I needed at the time.

It was five years after graduation and she had asked me what I was doing with my life. I told her that I wanted to enroll in graduate school. She laughed at me! She said, "Graduate school, are you kidding, you barely graduated from here!" She then asked me, "Why do you want to go to graduate school?" I said that I want to be a professor. She laughed at me again, and discouraged me from even applying to graduate school. I asked her for a chance, eventually she reluctantly agreed, and three years later I graduated at the top of the class from graduate school. I started teaching in my last semester of graduate school, and actually cashed my first check as a professor before I graduated. Two days after graduating from graduate school I was hired as a professor at two universities. I have been teaching as a university professor for the last eighteen years. A few years ago I returned to my alma mater to teach as a professor, the same dean was still there, and I laugh at her every time I cash a check from that university! There Ain't no CAN'T.

The first day on the job for my first medical device sales job was at the company's national sales meeting. I knew no one except my hiring manager. The first night was the awards ceremony honoring and acknowledging the previous year's winners for sales quota achievement and other associated awards such as Rookie of the Year and Presidents Club. It was a very elaborate and "first-class" affair. I was so taken back by the camaraderie and the reverence that was paid to the award winners, that I knew from that moment that I wanted to be up on that stage someday as an award winner. The top award was the President's Pinnacle Award for Sales Quota Achievement. This award honored the number one salesperson in the country from the previous year. At this point there were forty-one salespeople spread across the fifty states. From the next day on I had set my sights on winning the President's Pinnacle Award.

There was one problem. My territory was the worst territory in the country. In last place, forty-one out of forty-one. It had been in last place for several years. Multiple sales people tried to turn the territory around, all eventually giving up and moving on to other opportunities. Then I showed up. I told the Regional Sales Manager the morning after the awards ceremony, the second day that I am on the job, that I am going to win the President's Pinnacle Award. He laughed at me, he said, "You have the worst territory in the country, you are in last place, and have been in last place for years, you CAN'T win the President's Pinnacle Award." I looked at this as a challenge, and it did not happen overnight, but sure enough five years later I was up there accepting the President's Pinnacle Award for Sales Quota Achievement. I was number one in the country in sales, set records for sales quota achievement, made the largest sale in the history of the company for our main product, and set records for consecutive months at being number one in sales. There Ain't no CAN'T.

A few years later I was working at another medical device company. I had an opportunity to sell my equipment at not just one hospital but an entire network of ten hospitals. At this time this was never accomplished in my territory or region. It was a one at a time sales cycle. The regional sales manager said, "You CAN'T do this, we don't sell our equipment to a network of hospitals in this region, we sell to one hospital at a time." Again, it did not happen overnight, but I received a purchase order for all ten hospitals, for over three hundred devices totaling close to one million dollars in annual sales of equipment and disposables. Closing this sale catapulted me to the top of their sales rankings and I was a President's Club Winner for Sales Quota Achievement for them as well. There Ain't no CAN'T!

At one point in my career I was selling surgical instruments to hospitals. The company strategy to surpass the sales quota was to look for hospitals that were expanding their Operating Room facilities. When a hospital expands the amount of Operating Rooms, they are in need for new surgical instruments, a lot of new surgical instruments. In the recent history of the company the salespeople who were successful all had one thing in common. They all sold instruments to hospitals who went through expansions. My territory was different, my territory was saturated and none of my hospitals were candidates for an expansion. I had to come with an alternative strategy. I decided to focus on my top twenty existing hospital accounts, as opposed to hunting for expansion opportunities. My sales manager disagreed, he said, "You CAN'T do it that way, to get over quota you need to focus on expansion accounts". Sure enough I was able to develop relationships with my existing customers, I enacted a problem solving approach that focused on their needs and by the end of the year I finished as the number one salesperson in my region, number one in the Eastern Zone, and number three in the entire country garnering admittance into that company's President's Club for Sales Quota Achievement. There Ain't no CAN'T.

At a very early age I fell in love with sports. I loved watching sports, analyzing sports, learning about the history of sports, memorizing sports statistics, but most important of all playing sports. I was better at the watching, analyzing, learning, and memorizing than I was at playing sports. I knew that I would have to work hard and practice to ever have a chance to play sports. It did not come easy to me, but this experience at an early age in life helped me to develop a work ethic that acted as a solid foundation for any of the success that I have had in my life.

From my very first organized sports team, "tee ball" in little league baseball, the coach noticed that I was slow running to first base. He was right, I was slow, and I heard this my entire sports life from tee ball, through my late twenties when I still played organized tackle football. I was slow and I got tired of hearing it. What did I do about it? I needed to be better at other aspects of playing sports, like being smarter than being faster.

I love the sport of football, and I am the son of a football coach. I have coached football at many levels and the only reason why I did not become a football coach is that you have to be insane to be a football coach, totally consumed in the life, with minimal distractions (family) outside of football. People ask me why I do not coach football, since my father was a great coach? I always give the same response, I do not coach because I am the son of a coach, and I did not want to make that type of commitment that would compromise the time that I wanted to spend with my family.

I was a student of the game, I suffered a head injury at the age of twelve and did not play for a few years. I ended up attending my father's practices and games, he was a High School coach, and I would watch and analyze the team. I started compiling statistics during each game and informing the coaching staff of tendencies identifying which plays were successful and which were not. This was unheard of at the time, especially for a twelve year old. I began to understand football inside and out. I might have been slow, but I was smart. By the time I got to high school my head injury cleared up and I got the bug to play again, only now I wanted to play quarterback. I was immediately shot down, quarterback, you? You are too slow and you CAN'T play quarterback. I knew that I was too slow and I knew that I had to get better at the other aspects of my game. Nobody was smarter than me, so I used my intellectual ability and put it to work memorizing everything about learning the position of quarterback, from plays and formations, to analyzing defenses. I memorized the playbook and knew the assignments of all eleven players on offense for every play in the playbook.

Identifying strengths and weaknesses is a common strategy that can lead to success. Once identified, too many people focus on the weakness because a weakness is something that needs to be improved. If you are focusing on your weaknesses you are neglecting your strengths. If you neglect your strengths eventually your strengths will be diminished. There is a reason why it is a weakness, disregard it and focus on your strengths, if you do so you can make your strength stronger. If you improve your strengths, the weaknesses can become insignificant. I knew was too slow, and I was reminded of it every year, at every level, by every coach. Sure there were physical training exercises and routines that I could do to increase my speed, but at the end of the day I was too slow. I took the approach to make my strength stronger, and I decided to elevate my mental comprehension of playing the position of quarterback, and tried to become a smart quarterback, albeit a smart but still slow quarterback.

I was too slow to get recruited to play college football, but I did not let that stop me. I was told, "Are you kidding, you CAN'T play college football, you are too slow, especially to play quarterback" and I was actually laughed at when I told a high school coach that I wanted to play college football. I was given a chance as a walk on player, which is all that you can ever ask for in life, is for someone to give you a chance. On the first day of camp, I was given a chance, but I was on the bottom of the depth chart, in last place, number five out of five quarterbacks. By the time camp ended I moved up to number three with the other two quarterbacks being dismissed. I will never forget that day, I made the team, as a college quarterback.

I did not see any action in the early parts of the season, but midway through the season we were having our way with an opponent. The coach looked at me and said, "get in", I was not expecting to get into the game. I remember stepping on the field and began to be overcome by the moment. My whole life I was told that I was too slow, my whole life! Here I was not just playing college football, but playing at quarterback. As we got close to the end zone the coach sent in a play.

It was a handoff to one of the running backs. I looked at the running back and I said, "Sorry, this one is for me." On the play I RAN the ball in for a touchdown! That's right a rushing touchdown from the player who heard his entire life that he was too slow! It would have been great to throw a touchdown pass as a quarterback, but this was so sweet, it was symbolic, profound, and justice was served! At that point I was overcome with emotion and went into the biggest gyration of an end zone celebration that you could imagine. End zone celebrations can get out of hand, the proper way to act, is to act like you have been there before. I had never been there before, and I did not know if I would ever get back there again, so my emotions got the best of me. I spiked the ball so hard, I remember as if it was yesterday, spiking it so hard as if I was spiking it up the backside of every coach who told me that I was too slow to play quarterback. I ran off the field, as if I just won the Super Bowl, but you know what, it was my Super Bowl. I high fived and hand slapped every teammate, they were telling me to calm down, but no one could understand what I had to live with my entire life. I could not wait for the school paper, and when it came out I remember accumulating about fifty copies, because in the game summary it had listed my name, scoring a rushing touchdown! Do not ever, let anyone, anywhere, tell you that you can't do something. There Ain't no CAN'T.

I still have mountains to climb, I still have unfinished business that needs to be completed and I still hear the ringing in the back of my head, There Ain't no CAN'T. When Hall of Fame Coach Bill Parcells addressed his team after pulling off an upset and winning the Super Bowl he said to his team, "For the rest of your life, nobody can ever tell you that you can't do it, because you just did it"!

There Ain't no CAN'T.

There Ain't no CAN'T.

About Barchitta Consulting Inc.

Barchitta Consulting Inc. is a management consulting firm specializing in assisting corporations maximize their sales and marketing objectives. They can customize a training curriculum to meet the needs of your sales department. Seminar topics include:

- Motivational Speaking
- Sales Training Programs
- Managing Customer Relationships
- Understanding the Sales Process
- Shortening the Sales Cycle
- Why Customers Buy
- Time Management
- How to structure a Sales Force

Visit them on the web at: www.barchittaconsulting.com

Endnotes

1   Conlin, M. (2005). The easiest commute of all. *Business Week,*
    December 12,2005, P. 79.
2   McCune, J. (1998). Telecommuting revisited. *Management Review,*
    February 1998, P. 13.
3   Bartol, K. (1999). Reframing sales force compensation systems: An
    agency theory based performance management perspective. *Journal
    of Personal Selling and Sales Management,* 19(3).
4   Bartol, K. (1999). Reframing sales force compensation systems: An
    agency theory based performance management perspective. *Journal
    of Personal Selling and Sales Management,* 19(3).
5   Bartol, K. (1999). Reframing sales force compensation systems: An
    agency theory based performance management perspective. *Journal
    of Personal Selling and Sales Management,* 19(3).
6   Eisenhardt, K. (1988). Agency and institutional theory explanations: The
    case of retail sales compensation. *Academy of Management Journal,* 31(3).
7   Eisenhardt, K. (1988). Agency and institutional theory explanations: The
    case of retail sales compensation. *Academy of Management Journal,* 31(3).
8   Basu, A., et al. (1986). Sales force compensation plans: An agency
    theoretic perspective. *Marketing Science,* 4.
9   Ganzel, R. (1998). What's wrong with pay for performance? *Training,*
    35(12).
10 Ogbuehi, A., & Sharma, V. (1999). Redefining industrial sales force roles
    in a challenging environment: Strategic issues in selection, training,
    and management. *Journal of Marketing Theory and Practice,*7 (1).
11 Ogbuehi, A., & Sharma, V. (1999). Redefining industrial sales force roles
    in a challenging environment: Strategic issues in selection, training,
    and management. *Journal of Marketing Theory and Practice,*7 (1).

[12] Ingram, T., & Laforge, R. (1989). Sales Management: Analysis and decision making. The Dryden Press, Chicago, Illinois.

[13] Zemke, R. (1985). The systems approach: A nice theory, but.... *Training*, Vol. 22.

[14] Erffmeyer, R., Russ, R., & Hair, J. (1998). Needs assessment and evaluation in sales training programs. *Journal of Personal Selling and Sales Management*, 11(1).

[15] Erffmeyer, R., Russ, R., & Hair, J. (1998). Needs assessment and evaluation in sales training programs. *Journal of Personal Selling and Sales Management*, 11(1).

[16] Erffmeyer, R., Russ, R., & Hair, J. (1998). Needs assessment and evaluation in sales training programs. *Journal of Personal Selling and Sales Management*, 11(1).

[17] Stanton, W., & Buskirk, R. (1987). Management of the sales force. Irwin, Homewood, Illinois.

[18] Knowles, M. (1987). Adult learning, training and development handbook. McGraw-Hill Inc., New York, New York.

[19] Anderson, R., Mehta, R., & Strong, J. (1997). An empirical investigation of sales management training programs for sales managers. *Journal of Personal Selling and Sales Management*, 17(3).

[20] Anderson, R., Mehta, R., & Strong, J. (1997). An empirical investigation of sales management training programs for sales managers. *Journal of Personal Selling and Sales Management*, 17(3).

[21] Honeycutt, E., Ford, J., & Rao, C. (1995). Sales training: Executives' research needs. *Journal of Personal Selling and Sales Management*, 35(2).

[22] Honeycutt, E., Ford, J., & Rao, C. (1995). Sales training: Executives' research needs. *Journal of Personal Selling and Sales Management*, 35(2).

[23] Knowles, M. (1987). Adult learning, training and development handbook. McGraw-Hill Inc., New York, New York.

[24] Kohli, A., Tassadduq, S., Challagalla, G. (1998). Learning and performance orientation of salespeople: The role of supervisors. *Journal of Marketing Research*, 35(2).

[25] Keenan, W. (1990). Are you overspending on training? *Sales and Marketing Management*, (1).

[26] Rest, J. (1979). Revised manual for the defining issues test: An objective test of moral judgment development. *Minnesota Moral Research Project*, Minneapolis, Minnesota.

27   Harrington, S. (1991). What corporate America is teaching about ethics, *Academy of Management Executives,* 5(1).

28   Webster, F. (1992). The changing role of marketing in the corporation. *Journal of Marketing,* 56(4) p. 1-17.

29   Wilson, D. (2000). Deep relationships: The case of the vanishing salesperson. *Journal of Personal Selling and Sales Management,* 20(1) p.53-61.

30   Wilson, D. (2000). Deep relationships: The case of the vanishing salesperson. *Journal of Personal Selling and Sales Management,* 20(1) p.53-61.

31   Saxe, R., &Weitz, B. (1982). The SOCO scale: A measure of the customer orientation of salespeople. *Journal of Marketing Research,* 19(8) p.343-351.

32   Jolson, M. (1997). Broadening the scope of relationship selling. *Journal of Personal Selling and Sales Management,* 17(3) p.75-89.

33   Manning, G., Reece, B. (1995). *Selling Today.* Upper Saddle River, NJ: Prentice Hall Inc.

34   Berry, L. (1995). Relationship marketing of services-growing interest, emerging perspectives. *Journal of Academy of Marketing Science,* 23(4) p. 236-245.

Payne, A., Christopher, M., Clark, M., & Peck, H. (1995). Relationship marketing-key concepts. In: Relationship marketing for competitive advantage: Winning and keeping customers. Oxford: Butterworth-Heineman.

Dwyer, A., Schurr, P., & Oh, S. (1987). Developing buyer-seller relationships. *Journal of Marketing,* 51(4) p.11-27.

Callahan, M. 91992). Tending the sales relationship. *Training and Development,*12, 31.

35   Czepiel, J. (1990). Service encounters and service relationships: Implications for research. *Journal of Business Research,* 20 p. 13-21.

36   Dwyer, A., Schurr, P., & Oh, S. (1987). Developing buyer-seller relationships. *Journal of Marketing,* 51(4) p.11-27.

37   Day, G. (2000). Managing market relationships. *Journal of the Academy of Marketing Science,* 28(4) p. 24-30.

Fontenot, R., Wilson, E. (1997). Relational exchange: A review of selected models for prediction matrix of relationship activities. *Journal of Business Research,* 39(1) p.5-12.

Garbarino, E., Johnson, M. (1999). The different rules of satisfaction, trust, and commitment in customer relationships. *Journal of Marketing,* 63(2) p. 70-87.

Jolson, M. (1997). Broadening the scope of relationship selling. *Journal of Personal Selling and Sales Management,* 17(3) p.75-89.

[38] Williams. M., Attaway, J. (1996). Exploring salesperson's customer orientation as mediator of organizational culture's influence on buyer-seller relationships. *Journal of Personal Selling and Sales Management,* 16(3) p. 33-52.

[39] Anderson, J. (1995). Relationships in business markets: Exchange episodes, value creation, and their empirical assessment. *Journal of the Academy of Marketing Science,* 23(3) p. 351-357.

Jackson, B. (1985). Building customer relationships that last. *Harvard Business Review,* Nov-Dec. p. 120-128.

Williams. M., Attaway, J. (1996). Exploring salesperson's customer orientation as mediator of organizational culture's influence on buyer-seller relationships. *Journal of Personal Selling and Sales Management,* 16(3) p. 33-52.

Wilson, D. (2000). Deep relationships: The case of the vanishing salesperson. *Journal of Personal Selling and Sales Management,* 20(1) p.53-61.

[40] Garbarino, E., Johnson, M. (1999). The different rules of satisfaction, trust, and commitment in customer relationships. *Journal of Marketing,* 63(2) p. 70-87.

[41] Day, G. (2000). Managing market relationships. *Journal of the Academy of Marketing Science,* 28(4) p. 24-30.

[42] Dwyer, A., Schurr, P., & Oh, S. (1987). Developing buyer-seller relationships. *Journal of Marketing,* 51(4) p. 11-27.

[43] Frankwick, G., Porter, S., & Crosby, L. (2001). Dynamics of relationship selling: A longitudinal examination of changes in salesperson-customer relationship status. *Journal of Personal Selling and Sales Management,* 21(2) p. 135-146.

[44] McNeil, I., (1980). The new social contract, an inquiry into modern contractual relations. New Haven, CT: Yale University Press.

[45] Gao, T., Sirgy, M., & Bird, M. (2005). Enriching customer value research with a relational perspective: Evidence from an empirical investigation of organizational buyers' value perceptions. *Journal of Relationship Marketing,* 4(1/2) p. 21-42.

[46] Ganesan, S. (1994). Determinants of long-term orientation in buyer-seller relationships. *Journal of Marketing,* 58(4) p.1-19.

47   Berry. L. (1995). Relationship marketing of services-growing interest, emerging perspectives. *Journal of Academy of Marketing Science,* 23(4) p. 236-245.

Payne, A., Christopher, M., Clark, M., & Peck, H. (1995). Relationship marketing-key concepts. In: Relationship Marketing for Competitive Advantage: Winning and Keeping Customers. Oxford: Butterworth-Heineman.

48   Callahan, M. (1992) Tending the sales relationship. *Training and Development,* 12 p. 31.

49   Perrault, W., & McCarthy, E. (2002). *Basic Marketing: A Global-managerial Approach,* Chicago: Irwin.

50   Weitz, B., & Bradford, K. (1999). Personal Selling and sales management: A relationship marketing perspective. *Journal of the Academy of Marketing Science,* 27 (Spring), p. 241-254.

51   Jolson, M. (1997). Broadening the scope of relationship selling. *Journal of Personal Selling and Sales Management,* 17(3) p.75-89.

52   Doyle, S., & Roth, G. (1992). Selling and sales management in action: The use of insight coaching to improve relationship selling. *Journal of Personal Selling and Sales Management,* 12(1) p. 59-64.

53   Brooksbank, R. (1995). The new model of personal selling: Micromarketing. *Journal of Personal Selling and Sales Management,* 15(2) p. 61-66.

54   Doyle, S., & Roth, G. (1992). Selling and sales management in action: The use of insight coaching to improve relationship selling. *Journal of Personal Selling and Sales Management,* 12(1) p. 59-64.

55   Reicheld, F., & Sasser, W. (1990). Zero defections: Quality comes to service. *Harvard Business Review,* Se[tember/October, p. 105-111.

56   Weitz, B., & Bradford, K. (1999). Personal Selling and sales management: A relationship marketing perspective. *Journal of the Academy of Marketing Science,* 27 (Spring), p. 241-254.

57   Weitz, B., & Bradford, K. (1999). Personal Selling and sales management: A relationship marketing perspective. *Journal of the Academy of Marketing Science,* 27 (Spring), p. 241-254.

58   Beverland, M. (2001). Contextual influences and the adoption and practice of relationship selling in a business-to-business setting: An exploratory study. *Journal of Personal Selling and Sales Management,* 21(3) p. 207-216.

Leigh, T., & Marshall, G. (2001). Research priorities in sales strategy and performance. *Journal of Personal Selling and Sales Management,* 21(2) p. 83-94.

[59] Williams, M. (1998). The influence of salespersons' customer orientation on buyer-seller relationship development. *Journal of Business & Industrial Management,* 13 (Spring), p. 271-287.

Ganesan, S. (1994). Determinants of long-term orientation in buyer-seller relationships. *Journal of Marketing,* 58(4) p.1-19.

[60] Gao, T., Sirgy, M., & Bird, M. (2005). Enriching customer value research with a relational perspective: Evidence from an empirical investigation of organizational buyers' value perceptions. *Journal of Relationship Marketing,* 4(1/2) p. 21-42.

[61] Dwyer, A., Schurr, P., & Oh, S. (1987). Developing buyer-seller relationships. *Journal of Marketing,* 51(4) p. 11-27.

Morgan, R., & Hunt, S. (1994). The commitment-trust theory of relationship marketing. *Journal of Marketing,* 58(3) p. 20.

Kumar, N., Scheer, L., & Steenkamp, J. (1995). The effects of supplier fairness on vulnerable resellers. *Journal of Marketing Research,* 32(1) p. 5-65.

Odekerken-Schroder, G., & Bloemer, J. (2004). Constraints and dedication as drivers for relationship commitment: An empirical study in a health-care context. *Journal of Relationship Marketing,* 3(1) p. 35.

Anderson, J., & Narus, J. (1990). A model of distributor firm and manufacturing firm working partnerships. *Journal of Marketing,* 54(1) p. 42-48.

[62] Wilson, D. (1995). An integrated model of buyer-seller relationships. *Journal of the Academy of Marketing Science,* 23(1) p. 335-345.

[63] Dwyer, A., Schurr, P., & Oh, S. (1987). Developing buyer-seller relationships. *Journal of Marketing,* 51(4) p. 11-27.

[64] Morgan, R., & Hunt, S. (1994). The commitment-trust theory of relationship marketing. *Journal of Marketing,* 58(3) p. 20.

[65] Dwyer, A., Schurr, P., & Oh, S. (1987). Developing buyer-seller relationships. *Journal of Marketing,* 51(4) p. 11-27.

[66] Parsons, A. (2002). What determines buyer-seller relationship quality? An investigation from the buyer's perspective. *Journal of Supply Chain Management,* 38(2) p. 4.

[67] Dwyer, A., Schurr, P., & Oh, S. (1987). Developing buyer-seller relationships. *Journal of Marketing,* 51(4) p. 11-27.

Morgan, R., & Hunt, S. (1994). The commitment-trust theory of relationship marketing. *Journal of Marketing*, 58(3) p. 20.

68 Anderson, R. (1996). Personal selling and sales management in the new millennium. *Journal of Personal Selling and Sales Management*, 16(3) p. 17-32.

69 Doney, P., & Cannon, J. (1997). An examination of the nature of trust in buyer-seller relationships. *Journal of Marketing*, 61(2) p. 35-51.

70 Morgan, R., & Hunt, S. (1994). The commitment-trust theory of relationship marketing. *Journal of Marketing*, 58(3) p. 20.

71 Morgan, R., & Hunt, S. (1994). The commitment-trust theory of relationship marketing. *Journal of Marketing*, 58(3) p. 20.

72 Schurr, P., & Ozanne, J. (1985). Influences on exchange processes: Buyers' preconceptions of a seller's trustworthiness and bargaining toughness. *Journal of Consumer Research*, 11(4) p. 939.

73 Ganesan, S. (1994). Determinants of long-term orientation in buyer-seller relationships. *Journal of Marketing*, 58(4) p.1-19.

74 Morgan, R., & Hunt, S. (1994). The commitment-trust theory of relationship marketing. *Journal of Marketing*, 58(3) p. 20.

75 Gao, T., Sirgy, M., & Bird, M. (2005). Enriching customer value research with a relational perspective: Evidence from an empirical investigation of organizational buyers' value perceptions. *Journal of Relationship Marketing*, 4(1/2) p. 21-42.

76 Gao, T., Sirgy, M., & Bird, M. (2005). Enriching customer value research with a relational perspective: Evidence from an empirical investigation of organizational buyers' value perceptions. *Journal of Relationship Marketing*, 4(1/2) p. 21-42.

77 Gao, T., Sirgy, M., & Bird, M. (2005). Enriching customer value research with a relational perspective: Evidence from an empirical investigation of organizational buyers' value perceptions. *Journal of Relationship Marketing*, 4(1/2) p. 21-42.

78 Dwyer, A., Schurr, P., & Oh, S. (1987). Developing buyer-seller relationships. *Journal of Marketing*, 51(4) p. 11-27.
Morgan, R., & Hunt, S. (1994). The commitment-trust theory of relationship marketing. *Journal of Marketing*, 58(3) p. 20.

79 Anderson, J., & Narus, J. (1990). A model of distributor firm and manufacturing firm working partnerships. *Journal of Marketing*, 54(1) p. 42-48.

[80] Bendapudi, N., & Leone, R. (2002). Managing business-to-business customer relationships following key contact employee turnover in a vendor firm. *Journal of Marketing,* 66(2) p. 83-101.

[81] Morgan, R., & Hunt, S. (1994). The commitment-trust theory of relationship marketing. *Journal of Marketing,* 58(3) p. 20.

[82] Fournier, S., Dobscha, S., & Glen, D. (1998). Preventing the premature death of relationship marketing. *Harvard Business Review,* 76 (Jan/Feb) p. 5-12.

[83] Dwyer, A., Schurr, P., & Oh, S. (1987). Developing buyer-seller relationships. *Journal of Marketing,* 51(4) p. 11-27.
Morgan, R., & Hunt, S. (1994). The commitment-trust theory of relationship marketing. *Journal of Marketing,* 58(3) p. 20.

[84] Doney, P., & Cannon, J. (1997). An examination of the nature of trust in buyer-seller relationships. *Journal of Marketing,* 61(2) p. 35-51.
Kumar, N., Scheer, L., & Steenkamp, J. (1995). The effects of supplier fairness on vulnerable resellers. *Journal of Marketing Research,* 32(1) p. 5-65.

[85] Doney, P., & Cannon, J. (1997). An examination of the nature of trust in buyer-seller relationships. *Journal of Marketing,* 61(2) p. 35-51.

[86] Doney, P., & Cannon, J. (1997). An examination of the nature of trust in buyer-seller relationships. *Journal of Marketing,* 61(2) p. 35-51.

[87] Swan, J., & Nolan, J. (1985). Gaining customer trust: A conceptual guide for the salesperson. *Journal of Personal Selling and Sales Management,* 5(2) p. 39-48.

[88] Bendapudi, N., & Leone, R. (2002). Managing business-to-business customer relationships following key contact employee turnover in a vendor firm. *Journal of Marketing,* 66(2) p. 83-101.

[89] Schiller, Z., (1992). Goodyear is gunning its marketing engine. *Business Week,* March 16, p. 42.

[90] Schurr, P., & Ozanne, J. (1985). Influences on exchange processes: Buyers' preconceptions of a seller's trustworthiness and bargaining toughness. *Journal of Consumer Research,* 11(4) p. 939.

[91] Anderson, J., & Narus, J. (1990). A model of distributor firm and manufacturing firm working partnerships. *Journal of Marketing,* 54(1) p. 42-48.

[92] Lages, C., Lages, C., & Lages, L. (2005). The RELQUAL scale: A measure of relationship quality in export market ventures. *Journal of Business Research,* 58(8) p. 10-40.

93   Claycomb, C., & Frankwick, G. (2004). A contingency perspective of communication, conflict resolution and buyer search effort in buyer-supplier relationships. *Journal of Supply Chain Management,* 40(1) p. 18.

94   Boles, J., Brashear, T., Bellenger, D., & Barksdale, H. (2000). Relationship selling behaviors: Antecedents and relationship with performance. *The Journal of Business & Industrial Marketing,* 15(2) p. 141.

95   Keillor, B., Parker, R., & Pettijohn, C. (1999). Sales force performance satisfaction and aspects of relational selling: Implications for sales managers. *Journal of Marketing Theory and Practice,* 7(1) p. 101-115.

96   Boles, J., Brashear, T., Bellenger, D., & Barksdale, H. (2000). Relationship selling behaviors: Antecedents and relationship with performance. *The Journal of Business & Industrial Marketing,* 15(2) p. 141.

97   Schultz, R., & Good, D. (2000). Impact of the consideration of future sales consequences and customer-oriented selling on long-term buyer-seller relationships. *Journal of Business & Industrial Marketing,* 15(4) p. 200-215.

98   Macintosh, G., Anglin, K., Szymanski, D., & Gentry, J. (1992). Relationship development in selling: A cognitive analysis. *Journal of Personal Selling and Sales Management,* 12(3) p. 23-34.

99   Saxe, R., &Weitz, B. (1982). The SOCO scale: A measure of the customer orientation of salespeople. *Journal of Marketing Research,* 19(8) p.343-351.

100 Brooksbank, R. (1995). The new model of personal selling: Micromarketing. *Journal of Personal Selling and Sales Management,* 15(2) p. 61-66.

101 Schwepker, C., (2003). Customer-oriented selling: A review, extension, and directions for future research. *Journal of Personal Selling and Sales Management,* 23(2) p. 151.

102 Duncan, T., & Moriarty, S. (1998). A communication-based marketing model for managing relationships. *Journal of Marketing,* 62(2) p. 1-13.

103 Monczka, K., Nichols, E., & Callahan, T. (1992). Value of supplier information in the decision process. *International Journal of Purchasing and Materials Management,* 28(2) p. 20-30.

104 Morgan, R., & Hunt, S. (1994). The commitment-trust theory of relationship marketing. *Journal of Marketing,* 58(3) p. 20.

105 Robinson, P., Faris, C., & Wind, Y. (1967). Understanding the industrial buyer. *Marketing Science Institute.*

[106] Webster, F., & Wind, Y. (1972). Organizational buying behavior. Prentice-Hall.

[107] Webster, F., & Wind, Y. (1972). Organizational buying behavior. Prentice-Hall.

[108] Webster, F., & Wind, Y. (1972). Organizational buying behavior. Prentice-Hall.

[109] Howard, J., & Sheth, J. (1969). The theory of buyer behavior.

[110] Bunn, M. (1993). Taxonomy of buying decision approaches. *Journal of Marketing*, 57(1) p. 38-56.

[111] Bunn, M. (1993). Taxonomy of buying decision approaches. *Journal of Marketing*, 57(1) p. 38-56.

[112] Bunn, M. (1993). Taxonomy of buying decision approaches. *Journal of Marketing*, 57(1) p. 38-56.

[113] Bunn, M. (1993). Taxonomy of buying decision approaches. *Journal of Marketing*, 57(1) p. 38-56.

[114] Howard, J., & Sheth, J. (1969). The theory of buyer behavior.

[115] Anderson E., Chu, W., & Weitz, B. (1987). Industrial purchasing: An empirical exploration of the buyclass framework. *Journal of Marketing*, 51(3).

[116] Robinson, P., Faris, C., & Wind, Y. (1967). Understanding the industrial buyer. *Marketing Science Institute.*

[117] Webster, F., & Wind, Y. (1972). Organizational buying behavior. Prentice-Hall.

[118] Ozanne U., & Churchill, G. (1968). Adoption research: Information sources in the industrial purchase decision. Proceedings from Fall Conference of the American Marketing Association.

[119] Webster, F., & Wind, Y. (1972). Organizational buying behavior. Prentice-Hall.

[120] Connolly, T. (1976). Some conceptual and methodological issues in expectancy models of work performance motivation. *Academy of Management, Academy of Management Review*, 1(4) p. 37-38.

Behling, O., & Starke, F. (1973). The postulates of expectancy theory. *Academy of Management Journal*, 16(3) p. 373-375.

Reinharth, L., & Wahba, M. (1975). As a predictor of work motivation, effort expenditure, and job performance. *Academy of Management Journal*, 18(3) p. 520-521.

[121] Vroom, V. (1964). Work and motivation. John Wiley and Sons, New York.

122 Vroom, V. (1964). Work and motivation. John Wiley and Sons, New York.

123 Behling, O., & Starke, F. (1973). The postulates of expectancy theory. *Academy of Management Journal,* 16(3) p. 373-375.

124 Vroom, V. (1964). Work and motivation. John Wiley and Sons, New York.

125 Reinharth, L., & Wahba, M. (1975). As a predictor of work motivation, effort expenditure, and job performance. *Academy of Management Journal,* 18(3) p. 520-521.

126 Reinharth, L., & Wahba, M. (1975). As a predictor of work motivation, effort expenditure, and job performance. *Academy of Management Journal,* 18(3) p. 520-521.

127 Vroom, V. (1964). Work and motivation. John Wiley and Sons, New York.

128 DeCarlo, T., Teas, K., & McElroy, J. (1997). Salesperson attribution process and the formation of expectancy estimates. *Journal of Personal Selling and Sales Management,* 17(3).

129 Connolly, T. (1976). Some conceptual and methodological issues in expectancy models of work performance motivation. *Academy of Management, Academy of Management Review,* 1(4) p. 37-38.

130 Brown, S., Cron, W., & Slocum, J. (1994). Effects of goal-oriented emotions on salesperson volitions, behavior, and performance: A longitudinal study. *Journal of Marketing,* 61(1) p. 39-50.

131 Gray, G., & Wert-Gray, S. (1999). Research note: Decision-making processes and formation of salespeople's expectancies, instrumentalities, and valences. *Journal of Personal Selling and Sales Management,* 19(3) p. 54.

132 Behling, O., & Starke, F. (1973). The postulates of expectancy theory. *Academy of Management Journal,* 16(3) p. 373-375.

133 Gray, G., & Wert-Gray, S. (1999). Research note: Decision-making processes and formation of salespeople's expectancies, instrumentalities, and valences. *Journal of Personal Selling and Sales Management,* 19(3) p. 54.

134 Van Erde, W., & Thierry, H. (1996). Vroom's expectancy models and work related criteria: A meta-analysis. *Journal of Applied Psychology,* 81(5) p. 576.

135 Vroom, V. (1964). Work and motivation. John Wiley and Sons, New York.

[136] Van Erde, W., & Thierry, H. (1996). Vroom's expectancy models and work related criteria: A meta-analysis. *Journal of Applied Psychology,* 81(5) p. 576.

[137] Ingram, T., Lee, K., & Skinner, S. (1989). An empirical assessment of salesperson motivation, commitment, and job outcomes. *Journal of Personal Selling and Sales Management,* 9(3) p. 25-33.

[138] Kohli, A. (1985). Some unexplored supervisory behaviors and their influence on salesperson's role clarity, specific self-esteem, job satisfaction, and motivation. *Journal of Marketing Research,* 22(11) p. 43.

[139] Johnston, W., & Kim, K. (1994). Performance attribution, and expectancy linkages in personal selling. *Journal of Marketing,* 58(4) p. 68-81.

[140] Isaac, R., Zerbe, W., & Pitt, D. (2001). Leadership and motivation: The effective application of expectancy theory. *Journal of Managerial Issues,* 13(2) p. 212-215.

[141] Walker, O., Churchill, G., & Ford, N. (1977). Motivation and performance in industrial selling: Present knowledge and needed research. *Journal of Marketing Research,* 14(5) p. 156-168.

[142] Vroom, V. (1964). Work and motivation. John Wiley and Sons, New York.

[143] Walker, O., Churchill, G., & Ford, N. (1977). Motivation and performance in industrial selling: Present knowledge and needed research. *Journal of Marketing Research,* 14(5) p. 156-168.

[144] Kissan, J., & Kilwani, M. (1998). The role of bonus pay in sales force compensation plans. *Industrial Marketing Management,* 27(2).

[145] Kissan, J., & Kilwani, M. (1998). The role of bonus pay in sales force compensation plans. *Industrial Marketing Management,* 27(2).

[146] DeCarlo, T., Teas, K., & McElroy, J. (1997). Salesperson attribution process and the formation of expectancy estimates. *Journal of Personal Selling and Sales Management,* 17(3).

[147] DeCarlo, T., Teas, K., & McElroy, J. (1997). Salesperson attribution process and the formation of expectancy estimates. *Journal of Personal Selling and Sales Management,* 17(3).

[148] DeCarlo, T., Teas, K., & McElroy, J. (1997). Salesperson attribution process and the formation of expectancy estimates. *Journal of Personal Selling and Sales Management,* 17(3).

[149] DeCarlo, T., Teas, K., & McElroy, J. (1997). Salesperson attribution process and the formation of expectancy estimates. *Journal of Personal Selling and Sales Management,* 17(3).

150 House, R., & Dessler, G. (1974). The path-goal theory of leadership: Some post hoc and a priori tests. Southern Illinois Publishing, Carbondale Illinois.

151 Herzberg, F., Mauser, B., & Snyderman, R. (1959). The motivation to work. John Wiley and Sons, New York.

152 Herzberg, F., Mauser, B., & Snyderman, R. (1959). The motivation to work. John Wiley and Sons, New York.

153 Darman, R., (1997). Selecting appropriate sales quota plan structures and quota setting procedures. *Journal of Personal Selling and Sales Management*, 17(1).

154 John, G., & Weitz, B. (1989). Sales force compensation: An empirical investigation of factors related to use of salary versus incentive compensation. *Journal of Marketing Research*, February.

155 Cooke, E., (1999). Control and motivation in sales management through the compensation plan. *Journal of Marketing Theory and Practice*, 7(1).

156 Winer, L., & Schiff, J. (1980). Industrial salespeople's views on motivation. *Industrial Marketing Management*, No. 9.

157 Tice, T. (1997). Managing compensation caps in key accounts. *Journal of Personal Selling and Sales Management*, 17(4).